Digital Advertising

Digital Advertising: Past, Present, and Future
By Creative Social

Edited by Patrick Burgoyne and
Daniele Fiandaca

Creative Social

Thanks

Thanks to everyone who has supported Creative Social since its inception, including every speaker, all our sponsors, and every single Social who has contributed to our continued success. You all continue to be an inspiration.

In addition, a big thanks to Laura Jordan Bambach, Flo Heiss, and Patrick Burgoyne – without you this book would never have happened.

Contents

About Creative Social ix
Introduction xi

PAST 1
When Computers Came with Soldering Irons 3
When the 12 KB GIF Banner Was King 9
From Alpha to Better: Online Advertising, from
Then till Now 13

PRESENT 21
Anarchy vs Mainstream 23
Small Is Beautiful: Doing Good Digital Integration
and the End of the Big Idea 33
What Would Bill Bernbach Think? 41
Would the Last Person to Leave Please Turn Out
the Enlightenment? 49
How Advertising Can Become a Friend Whose
Company You Enjoy, Rather Than Just an Annoying
Salesman Who Sticks His Foot in the Door 59
Why Don't You Just Switch Off Your Television
Set and Go and Do Something Less Boring Instead? 69
Sound in Digital Advertising 77
The Latin Spirit 83
When Sweden Rules the World 89

FUTURE   **99**
   Your Brand Is an Ape   **101**
   Is Peep Culture the New Pop Culture?   **109**
   The Filter   **115**
   Get Involved: How You Can Shape the Future
   of Digital Advertising   **119**
   Brands as People   **125**
   Behavioural Economics and What Lies Beyond   **129**
   Being Good   **133**
   Agency of the Future   **139**
   A Blast from the Past from the Future   **149**

APPENDIX: Author Biogs   **155**

About Creative Social

Creative Social was founded in 2004 as a collective of the world's most pioneering, interactive creative directors and business owners – a group of people who recognised that collaborating in this digital landscape is how we'll advance the industry and enjoy our life–work imbalance even more. Twice a year we meet up face-to-face, just 35 individuals each time (taken from a membership of over 150) – the perfect tribe and catalyst for movement. We have so far visited Amsterdam, Antwerp, Barcelona, Berlin, London, New York, Paris, San Francisco, Sao Paolo, Shanghai, and Stockholm. We have spoken at the Cannes Lions, Dubai Lynx, Eurobest, and Creative Review's Click in London, New York, and Singapore. This book is our latest initiative to educate, inspire, and promote the industry. We hope you enjoy it.

Read more at www.creativesocialblog.com or follow us at @creativesocial.

Mark Chalmers and Daniele Fiandaca, Co-founders Creative Social

Introduction
by Patrick Burgoyne

For an industry that claims to prize innovation and creativity above all else, advertising is surprisingly conservative – no more so than in its initial attitude to the internet.

In the late nineties, agencies that had become fat on television and print advertising saw little to detain themselves in this new medium. This was a world in which creative directors prided themselves on being computer illiterate: secretaries were expected to send emails just as previously they had typed letters. Creative departments banned Macs; inspiration was the preserve of the pad and the marker pen, while computers were a crutch for the unimaginative. Within creative departments themselves a strict hierarchy reigned. At the top of the creative tree was TV; some senior teams refused to write for anything else. So in 1994, when the first banner ad made an appearance on the *HotWired* website (for AT&T), it was no surprise that the average agency creative was less than enthused. A 468 by 60 pixel banner was an awfully long way from a million-pound budget and a ten-day shoot in Rio with Ridley. This wasn't what they had gotten into advertising for.

What we came to term "traditional agencies" – those cumbersome dinosaurs of the pre-GIF age – held their noses while a new breed of digital natives led the way. As Simon Waterfall describes in his essay, often the people running the new agencies were not from advertising backgrounds at all. They had grown up with computers. They spoke geek fluently. While traditional creatives looked askance at the creative limitations of the banner ad, those whose most treasured teenage possession had been a Commodore PET were entranced by its possibilities.

We should acknowledge, however, that aesthetically speaking, those traditional creatives may have had a point. The initial internet advertising gold rush saw all kinds of crimes – the pop-up, page takeovers – that cause many to still shudder at the memory. Favourite websites were littered with horribly intrusive, annoying, blinking and winking things whose sole purpose in life seemed to be to get in your way and slow you down. It was no accident that pop-up blockers became such popular additions to browsers. This was advertising that was uniquely intrusive. If I'm reading a newspaper, I can ignore the ad on the opposite page. I don't expect it to start creeping across what I'm reading until, infuriated, I have to slap it back to its lair. Let's be generous and put such excesses down to youthful enthusiasm.

In these early days, it was tempting to think that this new medium would, from the advertisers' point of view, work almost exactly the same way as had print, outdoor, and TV. Media owners had audiences, and advertisers paid to access those audiences because they couldn't reach them otherwise. Publishers breathed a sigh of relief; they could still sell ads, just as they had always done. All they needed was a crash course in the new vocabulary of click-throughs and pixels to replace column inches. Digital display ads were no more than electronic versions of the billboards that increasingly dominated our city streets or the pages of our magazines. The editorial content was the main event, with advertisers jostling at the margins for some crumbs from the table. Just like in the offline world, advertisers had to shout and jump up and down to be heard. Websites were just more space to be bought and sold.

A very comfortable business could be made in servicing this new world of skyscrapers and *multi purpose units* (MPUs). But danger lurked: would this new breed of agencies repeat the mistakes of their elders? Just as they eagerly castigated the traditional agencies for automatically suggesting a thirty-second ad as the solution, regardless of the client's problems, so the digital agencies too were in danger of relying by default on the banner ad. Traditional agencies were systemically predisposed to TV and print because they were set up to deliver them; digital agencies were doing the same. If you have a room full of programmers to feed, you need to keep them fully occupied.

But as the internet has matured, it has become increasingly obvious that this is a unique medium. Applying the logic of traditional media was attractive to media owners and advertisers and their agencies alike. But it is wrong.

Rather than adapting traditional advertising thinking to the new medium, the real opportunity lies in exploiting the unique properties of digital in all its many variants to communicate in an entirely new way. The essays in this book illustrate that the brightest thinkers in digital advertising are attuned to these possibilities. And increasingly, so are what we once disparaged as "traditional agencies" – many of which have been busily buying up the best digital talent in order to reinvent and re-equip themselves for the new age.

There are two key factors at play in this changing reality. First, the internet is a two-way medium. This makes it participatory rather than passively consumed. The masses can answer back. Brands beware: shout at consumers, and they will shout back. As the internet guru Jakob Nielsen has said, "The web is not a selling medium; it is a buying medium. It is user controlled, so the user controls, the user experiences."

Secondly, and of equal importance, this new medium is open to everyone. Pre-internet, media owners held the keys to the kingdom because they had the technical means to create and control access to audiences. A newspaper invests millions in reporting, printing, and distributing to create a community of readers. It then sells access to that audience via advertising. TV works in the same way. But on the internet, access to the audience is, theoretically, open to all. A plethora of new channels – whether they be search engines or Twitter or Facebook – offer brands alternative means of speaking directly to their customers and, in turn, hearing back from them.

Thus, the theory goes, we are moving to a postadvertising age, or rather an age in which what we think of in terms of advertising – communication from and with brands – becomes seamlessly embedded in our everyday lives rather than being clearly demarcated or fenced off as it is now. While this is a doomsday scenario for media owners in print or TV (but hugely profitable for digital media players such as Google), it is immensely exciting for advertising agencies. You might think that a postadvertising world would have no need for advertising agencies – and in the strictest sense you'd be right – but such a world will certainly need smart people to help brands communicate with consumers. It is a mistake to think that this will happen only through what we now think of as advertising. Advertising and marketing are not synonymous.

The essays in this book show how this new reality might work, through what Daniele Fiandaca calls the four Es: *education, entertainment, engagement,* and *exchanging value* (see page 140). Now that brands are operating on a level playing field in terms of competing for consumers' attention, they will have to up their games. In the old media, money allowed brands to bully their way in front of an audience. Once there, brands could browbeat consumers into buying their products – call it the Cillit Bang Theory. This method has only limited effectiveness online. Instead, brands must offer some kind of reward to those spending time with them – a notion of "value exchange" that Chris Clarke, in his essay in this book, terms "the fundamental principle of the new advertising."

"In a world of consumer control," he notes, "brands are learning the humility to behave more like people than didactic organisations. Those that get it right provide a powerful value exchange based on a real understanding of what they can offer relative to their audience and communication objectives. Such brands are able to create engaging brand experiences with the potential to enrich people's lives."

So the new advertising has the potential to address one of the annoyances of advertising – its relentless hectoring – but what of the big one? What of the at times unprincipled manipulation that has cast advertising as public enemy number one in the eyes of many activists?

If, in this supposedly postadvertising world, it is no longer so easy to spot when we are being sold to, won't the degree of manipulation become ever more troubling? The relentless commercialisation of our lives is potentially hugely problematic. The idea that there might not be any form of entertainment that does not involve us being sold to in some way is, frankly, nightmarish.

On page 134, Johnny Vulkan asserts that "the generations born digital have a unique opportunity compared with those that preceded them because of a very simple shift: the world of commercial communication is no longer one way." The hope is that the two-way nature of the internet will ensure that brands' behaviours are effectively policed by consumers themselves, with those responsible for excesses quickly named and shamed. Consumers, Vulkan writes, are now armed with "the ability to research and question, to publish and provoke, that leads to the truth, because lying, skimping, shirking a responsibility, or denying a truthful allegation is simply no longer an option. You'll be found out." This vigilance will result in better products and services, which, from an agency's point of view "require us to simply connect people to them rather than batter them into submission or worry them into purchases."

This notion of the advertising agency as facilitator suggests a different role for the agency creative in this new world. In the old days, a creative in advertising made things: short films called commercials, printed paper to be pasted on billboards, radio ads. This kind of artifact-based advertising is steadily being replaced by the creation of systems. Advertising agencies will soon devise frameworks for information exchange, which will be open-ended and ongoing.

There's a parallel here with the differences between publishing in print and publishing online. A printed magazine is an object. It is manufactured, distributed, and sold, just like a pair of trousers or a box of soap powder. But smart publishers have realised that they are not in the business of selling ink on paper; rather, they are in the business of providing information. The printed page is (was) just the most appropriate means of delivering that information. That is not necessarily the case any longer. Many magazines are looking towards a wholly digital future.

Publishing a magazine online, however, is a very different proposition from publishing in print. Magazine websites are like machines. They need constant fuelling and attention. The fuel – the stories, the content – goes in one end. It mixes with the readership, ignites, and starts the whole thing chugging along. Those who used to be called editors are now engaged in constant supervision of the gauges: traffic falling off over here means some more fuel needs to be added, perhaps a comment stream over there is taking a discussion in an unwelcome direction and needs some of the heat taken out of it through moderation. It never ends. The machine must be constantly tended. And the contribution of the readership is as important as that of the editorial team.

So it can be with advertising. It is no longer about set-piece campaigns but about long-term, ongoing relationships between brands and consumers. Traditional properties such as commercials feed into the flow – they are the fuel for the machines – but the machine itself needs constant attention via social media.

In this move towards systems rather than artifacts, agencies need to find an appropriate way of being paid. They need to be paid for the true value of their contribution to a business, not just the time they spend on an idea – a problem several of the writers in these pages address.

This latter point is an issue for the entire advertising business, not just the digital wing. Perhaps because the internet is in the vanguard of our changing communication methods and ways of doing business, digital agencies have been at the forefront of thinking on this and many other issues facing the advertising industry. You are holding in your hands the evidence of that. The way in which this book came into being further illustrates the point. Creative Social is a coalition of the leading creative figures in the digital advertising business. It was not founded to make profit; rather its intentions are merely to promote knowledge and understanding in its chosen field. It comes out of the collaborative spirit of the internet that respects shared knowledge and community rather than the competitive culture of traditional advertising.

Creative Social's members share a very real belief that the future is in their hands. They believe that their chosen medium has the answers to the industry's many problems and that a future in which advertising is not reviled but actually celebrated for how it helps us live our lives can become a reality.

PAST

When Computers Came with Soldering Irons
by Simon Waterfall

You cannot undo invention. There is no Ctrl Z. Technology does not flow backwards. Children of ours will one day flip through our dusty photo albums and complain that the batteries are flat and the images don't zoom or flip. I'm thirty-nine. In just my half-lifetime, the void has opened up and here we are in the 01010101 age.

Technology has always had a rawness to it: the new comes straight from the minds of those who invent it, unpackaged, direct from those who live and breathe it. There is nothing to compare it to, no market to compete against. It is necessarily imperfect. With reckless abandon, underdeveloped social skills, and bad caffeine habits, our digital age was made real (or, rather, virtual).

It springs from many fields crashing together, at a time when invention could be done in sheds, with no money, and with friends rather than business partners and financial backing. They were *all* amateurs; there were no professionals. It was about technology, maths, electronics, and kids showing off to one another. Their stories are remarkably similar: William Hewlett and David Packard soldering hardware in a garage, Steve Jobs and Steve Wozniak tapping and hacking away in the Homebrew Computer Club. I started in my grandfather's workshop, piled high with lathes, pillar drills, oxyacetylene tanks, and, one day, a new tool. I had no idea what it did, how it turned on, or why it was sat on a coffee trolley stolen from the kitchen (Grandma wouldn't let tools in the house).

It was my first computer, a Commodore PET, and it was amazing. It was like nothing I had ever seen, touched, or played with before: a totally new breed of animal. And like any other new pet, you had to feed it and teach it, but every night, when you turned it off, the good stuff that made it work leaked out and you had to start again fresh in the morning. It wasn't house-trained, which I guess is why Grandma banished it to the shop. Made of metal, it was so cold in the mornings that I remember my flesh sticking to it as I typed. The only mouse in the workshop ignored it, as it did all the inedible junk in there. It was like a kid's game. There was no purpose to it; you had to make one up. It could, well, bleep and:

```
10 print "simon"
20 goto 10
```

Getting stuff into it was the hard part. I can remember a game called Eliza that came on a tape. After several attempts to load it by altering the volume levels on the side of a mono tape player, you could ask the PET things and it would answer with witty comebacks and quips – the beta version of Subservient Chicken. We thought this was fantastic: it suddenly made this hunk of metal and plastic useful and playful. It had started to become a real pet. My grandfather and I loved it. He never held me back. He was like another kid – a novice without boundaries. We had no fear that we would break it or screw it up (though he would never, ever swear, and I now make up for his deficiency and burn his blasphemy credits with fucking abandonment when it comes to malfunctioning technology).

Tapes: the start of software and of memory. Now when we turned off the computer we could reclaim the work the next day, so we could learn, store, and recover. Then, one day, miracle of miracles, came semifloppies: 5 1/4 inch disks (imperial). In storage terms, the jump from tape to disk was the difference between a cup and a swimming pool. Now, how to make a single-sided double density into a double-sided double density... and save a pound or so? A hole-punch could cut the required notch on the other side of the plastic envelope – the first hack I can remember, and it was analogue.

What made a computer the best toy were the accessories – all the extra bits that you plugged into it or made up from kits. The latter arrived from America. You soldered them together using instructions written, drawn, and printed by the guy who made them in his American shed on a slightly different voltage. Things would often glow a little red, and the smell of hot plastic and smoke was not uncommon. Not only did we have to build bits, but we had to program our own software from the back pages of magazines like *Popular Electronics.* Bugs... how come viruses are alive, and bugs died? They were the bane of my sister's life: she used to read out the endless lines of code as I tapped them in (peek, poke, sys4700). They never worked the first time, and you would spend a month of torment waiting to get the next issue of the magazine to get the bug fixes. This was the life cycle of a computer addict. Make, break, wait.

The next step up was the arrival of an Apple IIe: still no mouse, but the motherboard was easier to get to and plug bits into because the top lifted off. Underneath, moulded into the plastic, were the signatures of all the shed-heads at Apple who designed it. Even then Apple had a human touch that the rest of them missed. My dad was in the RAF and my grandpa flew his own small planes, so they bought the very first flight simulator in existence, with ASCII characters as the ground and trees. "It's so realistic!" they both crowed. My grandfather went on to add more reality by building a joystick from potentiometers, string, and springs. It took a weekend, but at the end of it, he fashioned peddles for pitch and yaw and told me to "hold on tight" when he looped the loop. It was fantastic. I was hooked on a green screen the size of a heart monitor and a speaker that was less musical than our doorbell.

By then I needed my own computer. They now came with colour and plugged into your own TV, and so moved from a tool in a shed to an entertainment device in the front room next to the Ferguson Videostar. The shift started an all-out war for computer domination, even in our farm village in Cambridgeshire where there were only thirty kids in a one-room school with two teachers, one doubling as the headmaster. Every computer house was different, ran different software, and had no consistency at all – and you thought browsers were bad. I had brand loyalty and so had a Commodore 64; the Pointons down the road had a BBC B micro, the Easthopes opposite had a Spectrum, and Marcus Pet had an Intellivision... fool. Of course I thought my beast was the fastest and the coolest. Stuck in a tiny village, I desperately needed friends outside to swap programs with (it wasn't illegal downloading – they came in the post. Remember, the internet hadn't been invented yet.)

With all this came a lifestyle that linked us geeks, the loners in bedrooms across the world. We had *Computer and Video Games* magazine and *BYTE,* which printed high-score charts so that you knew you weren't the only one out there – there were others who really got it too.

Instead of sweets, you could buy these games. A shop in Cambridge now sold them from a glass box that once held doughnuts and cakes; Pitfall and Attack of the Mutant Camels replaced the eclairs and macaroons. Tapes had reached their limits and floppy disks were in, but the memory of the computer was now restrictive. You filled 64 KB pretty quickly, even with expansion packs, and you had to do loads of game play with very little. It meant you kept your backgrounds down, kept sprites to a single square block and used repeated backgrounds, crushed the sound into loops.

Sound... oh my god, they had sound. I had grown up with bleeps and pings; now I had multiple channels, stereo. If things came from the left, then you heard them in the left speaker. That never happened with mono... oh my. The first soundtrack I can remember was Wheeling Wally. Oh, it was so good. When Hollywood looked in and started to do "integrated" launches, the Rambo game's theme tune stuck in my mind more than any shot in the film ever did. Explain?

All this advancement, but it was still in isolated pockets. Then, with my best mate, I invested in an acoustic coupler that you had to Velcro to the handset of the house phone (you had to be quiet in the room and not let Mum vacuum downstairs). This linked us into the big mainframe computers at the universities, where we joined all the *multi-user dungeons* (MUDs) and talked with other people. It was low-tech, but at last we were connected.

As my friend was only fifteen and I was sixteen, we were too young to have chequebooks or credit cards, so we decided to start a limited company. A loophole in the banking law meant that we could have a company chequebook and card. Awesome – we had credit! We started to sell our work, making extensions to the Basic language and then making our own games. It's what we had always done, but now it was a business. We started to find others who wanted to join, and before you knew it, we had an office with staff. We were working for Ocean, US Gold, Alligator, and other games publishers, but we had to sneak out of lessons to go for meetings, in our "retro" school uniforms.

So forward wind a year or two: I go to university to study industrial design, start a new company called Deepend with all the skills I pooled, the internet is just about to explode, the acoustic coupler gives way to a 24 KB modem, then 56 KB.... With the first web pages, I heard a lot of bitching about the restrictions, the lack of memory, the restricted palette. I just laughed. To me and my PET-owning contemporaries, this was huge. We had all these schoolboy skills that we acquired over years of playing in the shed, and all the problems that we faced then were now repeating themselves. I was back in the shed again, and I knew how to fix it with a soldering iron.

This really is the difference in my eyes between the digital industry and the advertising industry. The digital side has in the past always made tools. They built "things," whether they be play or practical, but they constructed things that were important in their own right – *end points,* I call 'em. The advertising side, which is amazing at telling stories and introducing us to the "new," are best at making signposts or creating reasons to go somewhere or buy something. Both industries have to work together hand in glove or mouse and mat, as you can't build a beautiful palace and then not tell anyone where it is. Selfishly, I believe that anyone who is creative in this day and age will be ultimately rewarded. The Net is full of people who curate rather than create. People who beg, borrow, or steal from the Net get unmasked very quickly, which is a problem for some corners of the advertising world, with their executive producers and dubious origins of inspiration. I predict that the fallout between the two will either kill or cure the divisions that have existed in the past. The people who build will always need an audience to sell their "warez" to. Go play nice together.

God bless you, Grandpa.
Goto 10.

When the 12 KB GIF Banner Was King
by Matt Powell

All the computers in the world are going to crash in just a few short weeks. In turn, our national security will be compromised, financial institutions will be brought to a halt, and our emergency services will be shut down. And all the planes will fall from the sky. And you won't be able to get any cash out.

That is pretty much the long and short of what I read in the newspaper on my way to my first day working in a digital ad agency. I'm still at that agency, and I'm still slightly disappointed that nothing exciting happened when the clocks struck midnight. The year was 1999, and the story (it must be coming back to you slowly) was the Y2K bug – the theory that all PCs would fail to cope with the date changing from 31 December 1999 to 1 January 2000. While the boffins got it hopelessly wrong, it serves as a reminder of how digitally primitive we all once were.

Stop and consider how much we've all changed since the turn of the millennium. Colour-screen mobiles, Google Street View, Wi-Fi–infused coffee shops, the iPad – these were all beyond our wildest dreams. Laptops were as thick as encyclopedias. Home broadband didn't even exist. Do I need to go on? A few knew that the internet was going to irreversibly change everyone's lives for the better, but a lot of people were cynical, even afraid of it.

When I think about how I felt on that first day at work, more than anything I remember a great sense of possibility. Back then small agencies had very little hierarchy or job definition, and no one really had any relevant experience to fall back on. Businesses were built on hope more than expectation. As it transpired, that hope was well placed.

As a consequence, in newly founded companies across London and beyond, there existed a creative free-for-all and banners were very much on the menu. A typical day for a creative back then involved getting up, getting in, grabbing a brief, thinking up an idea before lunch, crafting out a banner by the end of the afternoon, and – almost invariably – spending the evening in the pub. I'm simplifying things, of course, but it certainly felt as if the internet was a void waiting to be filled. It felt good.

The clients around at that time exaggerated the feeling too. So many new dot-com brands were starting up each week that banners soon became a kind of currency. To put it plainly, for a year or two in the late nineties, the GIF banner was king. And it ultimately changed the course of advertising forever.

The banner became a symbol of change, the standard bearer for two major shifts in the industry. Firstly, traditional agencies made the fatal error of ignoring the banners, caused by a combination of dismissing the format and a lack of willingness to change a regime that had served them well for decades. Secondly, the tight constraints that banner advertising posed drew out the best in a new breed of creative person: advertising grads, graphic designers, and entrepreneurs who knew it was now or never.

The challenge was to make a persuasive, coherent advert within a format shrouded in limitations. The GIF banner was just 468 pixels wide by 60 high. That's nearly an 8:1 aspect ratio – perfect for setting a line of copy but not much use for anything else. Then there was the 12 KB file size limit, barely enough to drop in a logotype and a background colour, leaving precious little space for a concept or graphic. Finally, there was a limit of just 256 colours, although working with just 40–50 colours was more like the truth. If those dimensions seem tedious, forgive me. I built hundreds of banners in those early years and just needed to write down the numbers for posterity. It's what many designers had etched on their minds.

As if those parameters weren't tough enough, there was also the pressure that clients suddenly had access to real campaign information. What had once been hard to quantify, now suddenly became maths, pure and simple. By dividing the number of clicks on an ad by the number of times the ad was seen – shazam! – clients suddenly "knew" if an idea had succeeded or failed. They weren't afraid to let you know either.

So was it all bad? Hell, no. For starters, what you saw on your screen was your end product – no plates, no wet proofs with colours that didn't match the Pantone swatch, no delays. You could animate (a tiny bit), and you could control the duration of each frame to 1/100th of a second. This, in addition to the creative freedom, was more than enough to sweeten the deal.

So we drew and wrote and presented and illustrated and animated – and it was a blast. The ideas gradually grew in complexity, but the parameters of the GIF banner remained the same, and creatives had to get clever at cutting corners. This in itself was an art form that got very little praise. Like a mountaineer cutting his shoelaces shorter to save a few grams from the weight of his feet, designers began removing imperceptible colours from the palette to save a little here and replacing a proper animation with a motion blur to save a little there. Happy days if you had creative OCD.

Spool forward over ten years (and those years have flown by), and suddenly the GIF banner barely gets a mention in the modern digital studio. It's the boring bit, the backup for the 2 per cent of people who have somehow managed to find a browser without a Flash plug-in. So why write this essay? It's because even if this is true, the GIF banner deserves a fond obituary before it slips from memory altogether.

Look at the banner's legacy: I doubt we'd be the creative directors we are today without all those early experiences. The GIF banner taught us a great deal – how to tell compact, concentrated stories to consumers and how to take advantage of the context of a web page. It helped us learn how to spot a stray pixel from a mile away and how to never accept defeat. Critically, it also left us with a permanent desire for hardware, budgets, and bandwidth to grow and grow and grow some more.

The 12 KB GIF banner may no longer be royalty, but it will forever be a benchmark of how far we have evolved. It will rightly be associated with a new chapter in advertising history and as such deserves to be treated as an icon.

From Alpha to Better:
Online Advertising, from Then till Now
by Andy Sandoz

Advertising has long been a contract. If you want the "good stuff" – *Skins, GQ, Star Wars* – it must be funded by the "bad stuff" – interruptions by freakishly happy, shouting people, spam and pre-rolls, and so on. But "good stuff" can be funded by more "good stuff," like Lady Gaga in Diet Coke curlers, Gmail, and Nike+. It just takes a little more effort. Online advertising has helped make this happen and helped make advertising as a whole better. Here is a timeline of its development:

ALPHA: 1995–2000

In 1995, I was twenty-two and Google was – negative three. I was using Photoshop 3, was two years away from my first dial-up connection, and didn't have a mobile – because mobiles were attached to cars.

But these were busy years for the internet. They gave us the first browsers, the first email spam – by a law firm – and the first banner ad, which ran on the companion website for a technology magazine. It was a small leap from selling ink on magazine pages to pixels on magazine websites.

The year 1995 also saw the launch of Amazon, eBay, and easyJet, plus the first dating site in Match.com and the first social network in Classmates. It's surprising to see the entrepreneurial and social foundations that would totally revolutionise advertising start so early.

BETA: 2000–1

Big business, these banner ads. They popped up over the "good stuff," and when blocked, popped under them. Sneaky. They came with their own language – *impressions* (amount of times an ad is shown), *cost per mille* (CPM), *click-through rate* (CTR) – and a staggeringly awful "success" CTR of 0.2 per cent.

By 2000 Google, now two years old, launched AdWords and, effectively, *search engine marketing* (SEM). Adwords watched what was being searched and answered with contextual adverts on the fly, thereby ensuring a more appropriate ad message based on user need. Clever – and very sneaky. This use of context is one of the most powerful additions to today's advertising.

However, to adland the concept was nerdy and unsophisticated, lacking the reach, gloss, and narrative of a broadcast model. Fair enough. The technology was still very new, and the thought of crashing your beautiful big idea into a 468 by 60 pixel, 12 KB flashing GIF simply wasn't very attractive in any sense of the word.

Instead online advertising caught the imagination of the Entrepreneur, the Geek, and the Youth – and in the best case, all three in one person. It was full of opportunity and experiment. By 2000 we had blogging, Napster, and Hot or Not. The internet began showing us it had an opinion, an attitude, and a sense of humour. Welcome to the Dot-Com Boom, grand ambition, and even grander website build. We all had a Hotmail account. Facebook was still four years away. There was no iPod.

Welcome to the Dot-Com Bust. The internet moves fast. It simply wasn't ready for such aggressive growth the first time around. Wikipedia, just born in our timeline, now tells me that the crash wiped out $5 trillion in market value of technology companies. However, this founding and spectacular failure did set the tone of the internet as a place of experimentation, possibility, and risk. Exciting. It also built the platform for tools and services, which were other powerful additions to today's advertising. Meanwhile, online advertising doggedly cranked out the banners and probably invented the *multiple-purpose unit* (MPU).

BETTER: 2001–5

Whilst the deep values of online society, sneaky intelligence (context), and service were being set, the internet rebooted. Tech advancement again led the way as infrastructure and rapid hardware/software advancements allowed online advertising to break out of its box. With the continued screwing of the established music industry via Last.fm and MySpace, alongside the first viral film of a chubby kid accidentally caught on camera wielding a broom handle/light saber (estimated views to date: over 1 billion), and the opportunity to escape to a Second Life involving clumsily bumping into things in bad animation, it all started to look like an interesting place.

The small company I joined around 2003 had an innovative microsite where users could leave video messages. It was full of short films of Japanese businessmen in meetings waving their hands – and weirdos waving their cocks. Not at the same time. YouTube was two years away, and don't even mention Chatroulette.

Microsites were rich and agile and for the first time supported a very high level of finish and interaction. Often they were the first collaborative effort between ad creatives, designers, and the new blended discipline of creative technologist. For brands it stretched the places where they could live and influence. For people (when they could find them – *search engine optimisation* [SEO] wasn't all that popular yet), microsites were deeply engaging and interactive experiences that were beginning to match the storytelling power and aesthetic of TV.

Video was a paradigm shift. The internet pipes were getting fat enough to shove film data down, and the "viral" phenomenon had begun, nicely demonstrated by our chubby Darth Maul earlier. Around this time I made my first interactive film, shot and directed in the basement of our agency. We created a site for the BBC that allowed the user to virtually feed a cocktail of drugs to a gurning, dancing clubber to teach and show – not patronise – teenagers about drug abuse. The interactivity was a new way to engage with this kind of message, the medium was the perfect way to target teens, and the execution was surprising, cool, and modern enough to share with friends.

In 2005 YouTube launched: dramatic chipmunks, laughing babies, people falling and/or failing, and Susan Boyle. I remember doing some prototype work on the concept of BBC iPlayer. Then the possibility of all that film seemed crackers. Today iPlayer shifts 12.5 GB per second of video, and YouTube has twenty hours of video uploaded every minute. YouTube is now interactive, and you can find HD and all of Channel 4's content there. YouTube can also auto-subtitle your film, which means it can search deep inside it. Wow!

BETTER 2.0: 2005–6

Hang on! We're at 2005 already and no mention of Facebook. You're right. Facebook launched in 2004 and was initially open just to universities. It really went public in 2006.

Somewhat pointlessly, (according to my dodgy maths)... Facebook had 9 million users in Sept 2006. By Feb 2010 it had 400 million.

391 million users in 1,278 days (3.5 years) = 305,947 new people have joined every day since the site's public launch. That should tell you all you need to know about social networks.

Anyway, so the internet was now behaving itself and looked pretty doing it. The people came along in large numbers and did stuff. Stuff we wouldn't have thought of. They got involved and changed everything. They downloaded (illegally), uploaded, rejected, accepted, commented, bitched, advised, and championed. They made friends, T-shirts, and films, and then shared them. Shared everything.

And online advertising? Whilst the possibilities atomised further via platforms such as microblogging, mash-ups, widgets, and co-creation, the role of advertising had become giving people interesting things to talk about and do. It gave them "stories" to be involved in. You can find a million essays about the "conversation of social media" online, so I'll let them pick up the weight here. In short, be interesting, be useful, be open.

Around 2006 we worked on a brief to re-engage a young audience with a large radio station, telling them that the radio had great DJs covering all genres. Our answer was to improve the established text listings showing a person's music tastes by providing a user-generated music "widget" that created a graphic statement on the person's MySpace about his or her tastes. Underneath this badge were streaming radio players connected to the station's ever-updating catalogue.

The users had already told us what music they liked in creating the widget, and so with that context we were able to serve a targeted radio player that accurately matched what users said they liked. Furthermore the users then showed off the DJs to their friends on their homepages, effectively doing our advertising with advocacy. It was part cool homepage badge and statement of identity within social networks, part tool that plays the music you said you like. The advertising was done afterward by use and experience. Show, don't tell.

BETTER 3.0: 2006–10

In late 2006, Twitter launched to too many column inches and shoulder shrugging, with people struggling to see the point. The point of Twitter wasn't about the brand or the 140-character limit. It was about the immediacy of the comment:

> All those little things all those people are saying right now
> +
> the fact that it's all contextual data that's immediately captured
> =
> a snapshot of now

You can create all kinds of interesting things with that opinion and data. Brands began listening to social media to hear what people were saying about them, first passively and then tentatively engaging in the conversations and finally curating them. What starts out as a database quickly can become a fan base. Brands now actively harness the power of this chatter. *Brand advocacy* (people doing the advertising for you by telling their friends) has become another massive addition to advertising that the internet has brought to the fore. All online advertising now has to inspire, curate, and manage this...in public.

In 2007 Apple launched the iPhone. Mobile had long threatened to be interesting. It tracked exactly the same curve as the internet, just faster. The iPhone was a paradigm shift; context on steroids. Your smartphone knows where you are through GPS or triangulation, and because it's on the internet, it knows a lot more than that. It knows what you think from Twitter, where you are supposed to be from your calendar, who your friends are from

Facebook, and what you like from your online shopping. Furthermore, it also knows a lot about the world: what's around the corner, when the train is coming, who a person is. The mobile is the bridge between the virtual and the real world – an augmented world. *Smart* is not the word.

What's more, the phone is open and developed by millions. Apps have provided yet another platform for brands to engage with their customers with tools, service, and entertainment. In 2008 Apple launched the App Store. One year later the billionth app was downloaded! User-generated content (UGC) in overdrive + e-commerce. Not only was the internet and online advertising changing the very nature of brand communications, it was also opening up new revenue streams.

And the phone is just the start. Many more smart "things" will come. My running shoes are smart with accelerometers, my table talks to my beer via radio-frequency identification (RFID), and my car is helping me to be green by monitoring and teaching me to drive better. At the time of this writing, we've just linked the data from a racing F1 car live to the website, giving fans a unique never-seen-before insight into a sport they love. It's a gift to the fans but also a software platform that changes the sport. It's definitely advertising – just a different kind.

Online advertising has come a long way since 1995. From initially mirroring the old practices of publishing, the banner ad has grown alongside the cultural revolution of the internet to fundamentally change brands and advertising as a whole. Digital is now at the heart of all communication. Brands no longer seek a database; they seek and curate a fan base.

As the medium improved technically, it grew socially, forcing brands to discover new ways of engaging and behaving as the power shifted much more to the consumer. The social power and activity, the creation of tools and services, and the context provided by technology and data have all made advertising better. The information online has become a power source. Like electricity, it now plugs into and powers all kinds of other technology with intelligence: your friends, your location, your health, your last purchase, the weather, language translations, the exchange rate, and so on. Initially with smartphones, now cars and tables and eventually yourself, the technology and possibilities continue to grow – and along with it (online) advertising, but with "good stuff."

PRESENT

Anarchy vs Mainstream
by Gustav Martner and Anders Gustafsson

Why not start with an email from Flo Heiss, asking us to contribute to this book:

> Gustav,
> We weren't 100 per cent sure what you wanted to cover in your piece, but we extracted that it is about the internet having changed from an anarchic place to a mainstream media.

Anarchy vs Mainstream?

Is this right?

OK. Flo had put his finger on it, even though I didn't realize it myself at the time. The internet was once an anarchic place. It was exciting. We were in the vanguard of a revolution. But now the internet is as much a part of mainstream media as TV and newspapers. The web has been built. The creative workshop has become a factory. The suits have taken over the party. Now what? Is there any room left for invention? For fun?

Feeling depressed, sad, and empty, I decided that I needed therapy. Perhaps an analyst could provide some answers. So I called my colleague Anders who, despite the late hour, was up working. He gave me a tip about a Virtual Shrink in good old PHP (to all the non-geeks out there, that's the scripting language *hypertext preprocessor*). This is how our first session unfolded.

Virtual Shrink: So... what seems to be the problem, young man?

Me: I've realized the fun is over. Once this business was so sweet, the coffee break was the only reminder of anything even remotely resembling a regular job.

Virtual Shrink: And now?

Me: When I look at myself in the mirror, I see a tired consultant. Eaten for breakfast every day.

Virtual Shrink: And perhaps you feel overpaid?

Me: Sure. That too. What happened? Why do I feel like this?

Virtual Shrink: Just take it easy. We'll get to the bottom of this. Time to shed some light on the matter with metaphors. You'll see – it'll make you feel much better. Let's start off with bicycles and "The Fine Art of Fine-Tuning."

Me: You're the boss. By the way, could I get an extra pillow for the couch over here?

Virtual Shrink: At the end of the eighteenth century, the French Count de Sivrac constructed the precursor to the bicycle. He called it the *célerifére*, or "fast runner." It was almost entirely made out of wood. One accelerated by moving one's legs and feet, like running while sitting down. In 1815, de Sivrac's invention was enhanced by the addition of steering handles. Later on came pedals and, in the following years, even more new developments.

Me: Now that's something.

Virtual Shrink: On 25 October 1994, *HotWired* published the world's first banner ad. It was bought by AT&T and looked miserable. Nevertheless, it was an innovative and groundbreaking idea, transferring an existing business model to a new medium. All of a sudden, you could buy internet ads the way you bought print ads.

Me: I've heard about website owners back then hiring "clickers" to get their rates up. Simply wonderful.

Virtual Shrink: Nothing is stronger than a perfectly timed idea like this. In the years that followed, we witnessed an explosion of innovative and interesting ad formats. All kinds of stuff.

Me: Yep. My personal favorites are (1) the billboard. Naming this cute little thing *billboard* is a great example of the delusions of grandeur that so often befell the ones who name digital occurrences. (2) The skyscraper: typographical enemy number one, useful only to those who aim at ads with copy such as "A cat sat in the hat" or "Hey! Buy!" Any longer and you're in trouble. (3) The scrollbar skyscraper: it's like your average skyscraper, but this one follows you like a street kid in India, until you get tired and take pity on it.

Virtual Shrink: Yes, but the interesting thing is that the banner is back. Smarter, more flexible, and definitely more interactive. Often a bit bigger. And if someone had wanted to know this in advance, I would have faxed him or her a copy of an interview I read with professor Jan Hult, bicycle historian. He said, "Nowadays there are more types of bikes than ever. But all of them, with a few exceptions, have got a frame, two wheels, pedals, and a chain. Other types of bikes have been tested on the market and failed. This is Darwinism on a technological level. The bike we've got today is the same as the prototype that arrived in 1885."

Me: Interesting. I've always thought of Facebook as a twenty-one-gear mountain bike.

Virtual Shrink: Ergo: count on the banner in the future – but with new neat details, smarter functions, and better formats in smaller weights. The only threat against the banner is if we fail to make it hot enough. Ugly and stupid ads will be sitting ducks. Look at the pop-up: more or less extinct today, exterminated by the deadly consumer – with a little help from Google's toolbox. The Puertasaurus of internet ads. Darwin would have been proud.

Me: And where do I fit in this image? As the Puertasaurus?

Virtual Shrink: No. But perhaps you dream of inventing a new bike – a revolutionary method of transportation on two wheels. If that's your ambition, perhaps you need to change your view on creativity.

Me: Or stop making banners?

Virtual Shrink: Or keep making banners, but start accepting the fact that you now are switching gears rather than moving the pedals.

Me: Ouch.

Virtual Shrink: There's a lot of beauty in changing gears.

Me: I still don't feel good.

Virtual Shrink: Well, I've got more. You've got kids these days, haven't you? Do they like pancakes?

Me: Sure.

Virtual Shrink: The internet has always been a place for subcultures – internet users were a subculture themselves to begin with. Remember the term *netizens*? Who isn't a netizen today? The word is obsolete. The internet is fully integrated with our lives. Using it isn't particularly exciting or identity forming. It's not that cyberpunk to Google a recipe for pancakes with a baby on your arm.

Me: It's not that cyberpunk to Google a pancake recipe, baby on arm or not. Period.

Virtual Shrink: Well. Let us discuss punk anyway – or more accurately, punk aesthetics. I'm very fond of punk, at least the visual expression of the first punk bands. The Ramones. Television. Bad Brains. Blondie. Just look at their style! But the punk uniform hasn't developed noticeably in the last twenty years. The power of innovation has left the genre, like an empty helium tank; the balloons are filled, and they've all flown away.

Me: Pow!

Virtual Shrink: With the internet becoming everyday, a bunch of conventions establish themselves. Suddenly there are habits and accepted procedures to follow, so innovation and mad, experimental science take a back seat. Before, imagination and the urge to explore strange new worlds came first. Today everyone is looking for experience instead! Experienced creatives. Experienced directors. Experienced programmers.

Me: Yuck. Tell me about it. With experience you get conservatism. Conservatism in advertising leads to fear. Fear leads to anger, anger to hate. This is the path to the dark side.

Virtual Shrink: And the identity that used to be dynamic and constantly reinventing itself has gone stiff. Maybe it's become a uniform, just like the punk uniform. But what's even worse is the fact that everyone puts their faith in authorities with proven experience. They suddenly run the show and get to take responsibility for their actions. It impedes development.

Me: Authorities?

Virtual Shrink: Early web entrepreneurs – like you and your Creative Social buddies.

Me: My ideas wear a uniform?

Virtual Shrink: Didn't you launch two sites in the same week called something ending in "o-gram"?

Me: …

Virtual Shrink: Forgive me. Ever heard about Descartes?

Me: Yeah, I'm afraid so. Isn't that the guy responsible for making our beautiful world so damn rational? "I think, therefore I am" and sucky stuff like that?

Virtual Shrink: *Cogito ergo sum.*

Me: If Descartes were in advertising, he'd never get a job at our place.

Virtual Shrink: He lived in seventeenth-century Europe. Thinker and scientist, half mathematician and half philosopher –

he studied everything from geometry and optics to astronomy and anatomy. One of his biggest accomplishments was figuring out the connection between geometry and algebra. Great, don't you think?

Me: Amazing.

Virtual Shrink: But how come Descartes succeeded where so many mathematicians failed? Well, the man wasn't a complete idiot. But apart from exceptional intellect, Descartes lived in a time when scientists studied anything they found interesting – totally cross-scientific, in other words. Descartes was one of them, and he also had a wealthy family supporting him without too many expectations. He could go about his business and study fresh, steamed pig hearts (to find a way to grow older than 100) and in the next minute solve an ancient Greek mathematical problem. Science was passionate and uncompromised. Ideals and morals decided scientific goals. Pretty far from where we are today. Personal ideals and sudden, totally random thoughts don't get that much space today – regardless of whether you're a scientist or a creative in digital media.

Me: There's not that much room for spontaneous and random ideas these days, no.

Virtual Shrink: When a niche expands like the one we're in, a need for experts within that niche emerges. The more experience, the bigger the need for niche expertise. The foundation is in place; now it's time to build the house.

Me: Web 2.0!

Virtual Shrink: … and individuals and agencies are finding their niches, again. That creates better quality overall – but maybe we're missing the big ideas. Hatching big ideas demands a comprehensive understanding that might be hard to obtain today.

Me: So, we're screwed? You've talked about bikes – pointless to improve. About punk aesthetics – deader than dead. About Descartes - the last generalist. Is there no hope?

Virtual Shrink: Of course there is – but you have to let go of the old. Nostalgia has no place in your industry. And work harder. Writing an essay about this is really kind of silly. You've got nothing to tell people about this business yet, have you?

Me: Good point. That actually makes me feel a bit better. But are you saying that there is no longer any need for innovation on a grand scale? That it will be incremental and small scale from now on? Details rather than big picture?

Virtual Shrink: No, not necessarily. But what does your heart tell you?

Me: Frankly, I'm not sure. Everything has gotten a bit too big. A bit too serious. And not that fun.

Virtual Shrink: Are you sure? I met this guy the other day, he's just been in the industry for one year and before that he was a gaming programmer. Bump mapping and artificial intelligence – heavy stuff. So I asked him if he didn't feel bored being in advertising all of a sudden, with limited time, space, and formats – so different from heavy programming in the gaming world. Do you know what the guy said?

Me: I do not. Tell me.

Virtual Shrink: He said that this is the time to be here. This is when it's all happening. It's all getting faster. Monitors and screens everywhere are getting integrated with online stuff, and issues like piracy and copyright are finally about to get – well, if not solved, at least somewhere. It all starts now.

Me: Really? That's pretty insightful. Maybe a bit naive, though.

Virtual Shrink: But apparently he saw things in a different way. Maybe that's exactly why you are here today. Perhaps it isn't about finding a new standard. How about going cross-scientific? Investigate by heart? Use that sought-after experience of yours to always keep in touch with why and how things became what they are today. Create great stuff – regardless of the angle. Just find the best idea – no matter where it came from. Have fun in front of your computer. Or anywhere else for that matter.

Me: Yeah. I actually feel better now. Who was that guy? Why did he visit? Doesn't seem like he needed therapy at all.

Virtual Shrink: No, actually he just added some cool features in my code repository. So next time, we can talk about the Clash and summer cottages!

Me: Sweet.

Small Is Beautiful: Doing Good Digital Integration and the End of the Big Idea
by Ale Lariu

You've spent the last five years trying to do "integrated" work; in other words, your TV ad, your press ad, and your website all look the same. You're very proud because you've just about mastered integration. Well, here's the bad news: you missed the point. A website is just the tip of the digital iceberg. The digital channel is now so fragmented that we need to start talking about how integration within digital is important. And it gets worse. A TV ad is probably no longer the best way to solve a client's problem. The answer may as well be an iPhone app or a new product launch. We need to stop thinking "campaigns" and start thinking how can we solve our clients' problems in a media-agnostic way.

But if we all follow some simple conventions, we can make the most of these new opportunities. Before we go into the dos and don'ts of digital integration, here are three starting points on the generic definition of *integration*. Please read the one most likely to be you:

1. You're new to advertising. Integration within advertising happens when you sell a brand's products and services across different channels (TV, print, radio, and digital) with a cohesive approach to problem solving that takes into consideration each channel's characteristics.
2. You already work in an agency. You probably know the drill. Just be aware that ideas can sometimes start quite small in different channels before reaching mass appeal. More on this later.
3. You're a client. Some of you are getting it right, and some of you are getting it wrong. So if you still think integration is your press ad put into a banner, please go back to point one and start again. And for those of you who still think an idea must come from a TV or print agency, you need to get out more.

Now let's stop with the generic and focus on the digital sphere. Good digital integration is making the most of every digital output independent of what country or culture the work is going to be shown in. When I say *digital channel*, I mean everything from mobile to an interactive digital display. And that's what's so exciting about this channel: it has many subchannels where data can be easily transferred from one to the other. What's on a billboard stays on the billboard, but what's on the web can be viewed on a mobile device and vice versa. And no, putting a URL in a billboard is not true integration.

From an agency, client, or more importantly, a consumer's perspective, digital integration is becoming increasingly important – so much so it should no longer be considered a niche area in the marketing mix. This is because consumer behaviour has changed as people are spending more time interacting with digital channels. This alone justifies the need for good digital integration.

So how can you make the most of digital integration? Here are some dos and don'ts for beginners, agencies, and clients.

DON'T

1. Don't do matching luggage; adapt an idea to a channel. Visuals around the same idea can change, and a digital ad does not have to look similar to the other campaign advertising. Sadly, or should I say fortunately, no one creative solution fits all.

2. Don't blindly trust focus groups – or at least not in the way you are used to. In old marketing, most notions of what the consumer liked in a product were second-guessed. Now it doesn't need to be; just ask them straight. Why not test a series of ideas online before they get "made" into final executions? It can be done.

   The other key point is that research might throw up something great for TV that might not be relevant for online. And even within online, a campaign could vary depending on the consumer's mindset; for example, the mindset when a consumer is logged into a bank site is totally different than when he or she is surfing for fun. Research needs to be fine-tuned within the digital channel.

   And finally, get over the fact that you don't know what people actually want. Instead, ask them. If you're testing an iPhone or an iPad app, get feedback from the iTunes stores. If you're testing a new product idea, get real-time sound bites on Twitter. Stop thinking that when a product, an idea, or even a campaign leaves your company and sets out into the real world, you're done with it. Fine-tuning your creation can be the best part of producing something.

3. Don't always go for mass reach; try lots of small clusters. Again, the holy grail always used to be mass approach: a TV ad that everyone saw and then a site that everyone knew. But take a look at social networking. If you just go there shouting about your product (no matter how nicely

you do it), people won't listen. You need to tap into individual behaviours. For example, can you tap into the fact that most people upload pictures of a night out or thank each other for being added to a group of friends? This will take time but will be worth it in the long run.

DO

1. Take risks and love being in beta. Don't sink all your money into one website that you think will solve everything. Experiment a little. Try lots of different types of behaviour within the digital context. Sounds like common sense, but not many people do it. Try something within mobile, for example. How about a mobile application for a makeup brand that recommends shades based on complexion and clothing? It has been done. The app doesn't necessarily need to be part of a website – just a neat little utility that works well when you have your phone with you rather than your computer.

2. Partner your ass off; sometimes a great idea is a great partnership idea. Yep, it's really hard to come up with something that has never been done before, so you either have to improve something that exists or partner your ass off. Every day new business ventures and technologies are born, so if you join forces the potential to create something completely innovative is huge. Every day of this remixing culture we are bombarded by amazing mash-ups that can elevate your brand to a different status. From tactical partnerships like PayPal and Facebook to more fun ones like using Twitter as the entry mechanic for a competition, think of all the untapped digital potential of start-ups and new technology. For example, a concert calendar AIR app that uses the music you like from your iTunes to recommend gigs. You guessed it – people have done it before.

And what does all this have to do with good digital integration? Well, if you exhausted your brand possibilities in many digital channels or they are simply not working as hard as you'd like, remixing and partnering up can be a great way to refresh your otherwise-tired social media ventures.

3. Refresh, refresh, refresh – maybe you'll create a phenomenon. Look around you. Loads of things are happening that might not immediately seem relevant to your brand or project. Start-ups, new technology, new behaviour – like flash mobs or Chatroulette – show that people are engaging with others in different ways all the time. Why not take that successful pattern of engagement and apply it to a part of your digital integration? Is there something you can learn about the success of flash mobs and apply it to something as random – and potentially boring – as e-commerce? The point is, you will not know until you try.

4. Earn their attention; don't pay for it. Everybody says it, but not many people do it. In this day and age, brands that earn attention have a higher level of engagement with consumers. After all, let's face it: banners and websites are pretty much templated channels now. Everybody in the communications industry should know how to make one. The more challenging approach is to come up with digital channels that collectively are going to grab people by the balls and not let them go. All your digital efforts should be geared towards being part of a person's life 24/7. So think about how you'll talk to people when they're not at their desks, when they're with friends, when they want to feel part of something. If you're a retailer, for example, you should use your site to inform people. But information and customer support can be doubled up on Twitter. Your employees can offer support in 140 characters, can't they?

5. Involve people – they like to talk. Let's say you have a great mobile app that offers people cool shit they can also get on your website, Twitter, and Facebook. Job done? Kinda. It would be much better if you could link all of those channels and let people talk to one another on all of them. So yes, let's make the most of Facebook Connect and Twitter @anywhere. It's much better for people to see what their friends like than a bunch of random users they don't know about. So whether you're selling something or launching a new product, think of ways your customers can take their friends with them and help spread the word. It's one of the best forms of free advertising out there.

6. Write briefs for specific digital engagements. It's no longer simply good enough to have a generic digital brief. Identifying a great problem is as good as solving the problem itself.

   What's right for a website that is targeting millions of people might not be right for a widget on a social networking platform. People think differently at different times of the day and depending on what platforms they're using. So try and get this thing right internally, and you'll be halfway there. For more specific tactical projects, it's amazing what a good brief can do.

7. Most importantly: don't be afraid to start small. You can find big opportunities in small ideas that start out in any of the marketing channels but specifically now within the digital space. You never know where a successful idea might start to come alive, so all the more reason to sprinkle the landscape with lots of them.

   So does this "start small" thing mean the end of the big idea? No. Making the most of every channel and making the most of every little opportunity within the digital channel only adds to the mix – perhaps in a more cost-effective way. Digital is a great place to start small, as it's not only easier to test ideas but also often cheaper. A great idea on Twitter, followed up by a series of small partnerships and a Flickr group can be as effective as buying online ads. Just don't think banners and microsites. Truly understand all the small digital opportunities and how to tap into them, and you might end up with something big.

What Would Bill Bernbach Think?
by Sam Ball and Dave Bedwood

Séance transcript

19:30, 6 March 2010, Kings Cross, London

Present: Dave Bedwood, Sam Ball, Marie Baresford

Objective: To contact and seek the wisdom of Bill Bernbach, father of modern advertising, who died in 1982. Has the internet fundamentally changed the principles of advertising? If he were alive today, how would he approach digital advertising?

Marie Baresford: (slowly) Is there anybody there?

(silence)

Marie Baresford: Is there anybody there?

Colonel Sanders: Hello, I'm Colonel Sanders. Who is this?

Marie Baresford: Is anybody else there?

Bill Bernbach: Hello, Bill Bernbach here. Who am I speaking to?

Sam Ball: (slightly startled) God, hello Mr Bernbach. My name is Sam Ball, and I'm here with Dave Bedwood. We're the creative partners of a digital advertising agency called Lean Mean Fighting Machine.

Bill Bernbach: What an absurdly stupid name, and what on Earth is digital advertising?

Sam Ball: I won't begin to explain the name, but we work in the world of advertising. Most of our adverts appear on the internet. Just to bring you up to speed, Bill, the internet is a huge connection of computers that spans the entire globe, enabling people to communicate, find out information, share photos, films, thoughts – all in an instant, anywhere in the world, without taking up any space or costing much money. Because people are spending so much time using their computers to do these things, advertisers now have another medium through which to talk to people.

Bill Bernbach: Have I been gone that long?

Dave Bedwood: Bill, we've got so many questions about life, death, God, the Universe... but seeing as we might not have much time, the most important thing we'd like to ask your opinion on is digital advertising. Do you think we need to rewrite the rule book since the advent of the internet?

(long silence, in which everyone in the room opens one eye)

Marie Beresford: Hello, Bill – could you respond? I know you're still here.

Bill Bernbach: Sorry, I was just looking at an old book of my quotes. Well, it doesn't sound to me like you need to rewrite the rules; rather, brands need to go back to the core creative philosophies. I remember the advent of TV. We were creating newspaper, poster, and radio ads at the time. The same conversations were ringing around the office: "Do we need to rethink how we go about doing great advertising? What is great advertising?"

Sam Ball: What were your conclusions?

Bill Bernbach: Let's put this into perspective. In the early fifties, only 10 per cent of homes had TV sets. By the midsixties, this figure rose to 95 per cent. America was young and optimistic, and there were exciting times ahead. The problem was that the old guard in charge of the advertising industry didn't know how to communicate with the new consumer effectively; they were still talking to people in a conventional way and treating them as idiots.

Sam Ball: Sorry to say, but some things haven't changed....

(long pause)

Bill Bernbach: Well, the great art director Helmut Krone had a good analogy about this kind of advertising. He likened it to being sold to by a man on your doorstep. If he shouted or treated you like you were an idiot or talked down to you, you naturally wouldn't buy anything from him. We tried to write ads on the new medium of TV in a way that was thoughtful, treating consumers with respect and persuading them with charm and wit. The skills needed for that turned out to be no different than the ones we were employing with our best radio and press work. I would guess that these would be the same skills I would employ on your internet.

Dave Bedwood: I remember a quote you had from that time, about the fact that it took millions of years for man's instincts to develop, so it will take millions more for them to vary. It's fashionable to talk about changing man. A communicator must be concerned with unchanging man, with—

Bill Bernbach: (abruptly interrupting) His obsessive drive to survive, to be admired, to succeed, to love, to take care of his own....

Dave Bedwood: Yes, sorry, they are your words.

Bill Bernbach: I still stick by that. Every era has the same problems. We had it with advancements in mass media like TV, but our philosophy was always to adapt your techniques to an idea, not an idea to your techniques. It looks like that might be even more important in your era.

Marie Beresford: Quite.

(Sam and Dave both open an eye and look at Marie and then each other.)

Dave Bedwood: (clears his throat) We feel that the internet is the next step in what you were trying to do, Bill. Essentially, your ads were trying to talk to people and create a dialogue on their terms, but what we have is the chance to actually have a dialogue. People can talk back and get involved. In the past, however successful your communications, it was always one way and passive. With our new technology, we can create work that goes beyond anything a passive medium like TV could offer.

Bill Bernbach: I take your point, and to a certain degree, I think you're right. I would certainly see the internet as an extension of where I wanted to take advertising. We were trying to create a dialogue. Yes, TV, print, poster are essentially one way, but to counter your point, I do think some of our best ads achieve this: they leave a gap for the consumer to fill in. By working out an ad, the consumer is interacting with it. I do see the power available to you today through the use of technology, but I'd warn you against believing that the core principles of advertising are not relevant.

Sam Ball: It's more that we think digital is different because the technology of the medium is so much more integral to how an idea can be expressed.

Bill Bernbach: But how you go about creating the right strategy, tone, insight, and message is exactly the same process if you wish to make a great TV ad or a great digital ad. How it is finally expressed differs because each medium gives a creative person different tools with which to paint the final picture.

Sam Ball: There is great debate at the moment as to who will own the future of advertising – the traditional agencies or the new digital agencies. What do you think about that?

Bill Bernbach: Well, at the heart of an effective creative philosophy is the belief that nothing is quite so powerful as an insight into human nature. What compulsions drive a man? What instincts dominate his actions, even though his language so often camouflages what really motivates him? This is the basis of any great advertising and, of course, has little to do with where or how the advertising appears. Wherever your consumer is, you need to speak to him in this way, via whatever medium. Whoever can manage to do that will own the future.

Dave Bedwood: We often say that a good joke in today's world could be seen in dozens of different media from a billboard to a text message to Twitter to a press ad or on a phone, but what matters most is how good that joke is. To write a good joke takes a lot of skill and understanding of your audience. Without that it isn't funny, and no one will laugh, remember, and pass it on.

(silence)

Bill Bernbach: I am sure that is one of my analogies, but I will let it slide. It's a good point and relevant whatever year it was originally said. Yes, you have fantastic technology, but it is only a conduit to the story, the idea. Those things, again, are powerful only if they are written in a way that touches the human psyche. The most difficult thing, as always, is not creating technology that allows you to share content; it is making content that is worth sharing.

Sam Ball: And how about the fact that people can now get involved in your advertising? Or ignore it altogether if they wish?

Bill Bernbach: How can they ignore it altogether?

Sam Ball: People are becoming more and more in control of their media and how they receive it. So for instance, with TV you can record it and play it back, skipping all the adverts if you like.

Bill Bernbach: How does the programming afford to be on air? Anyway, I think this is a natural progression, and to be frank, most of the advertising we used to have on TV was terrible – but that was because it wasn't made with the core creative philosophies I've been talking about. Whatever content you make today, as an advertiser you need to make sure it's good enough that the consumer wants to consume it. That, in my opinion, happens only when it's written from the standpoint I've laid out.

Dave Bedwood: How do you combat the rising power of consumers when they can use the internet to express their opinions, make their voices heard, and damage an advertising campaign and product?

Bill Bernbach: If there really is two-way communication because of the internet, then I feel that there is even more need to write advertising that adheres to these core philosophies. Anything that doesn't will rightly become a victim of this consumer power. Surely, we will get less bad work...?

Dave Bedwood: Do you wish you were in advertising today?

Bill Bernbach: Well, I'd be alive, so yes.... It does sound very interesting. My agency always wanted to create in the latest idiom. In my era, that was TV; in yours, it's digital media. Like the sixties, it sounds like it's a unique time for advertising creativity. In my day, it was a change of mentality that allowed greater freedom and the letting go of old ways. Now it sounds like technology is provoking this creative revolution.

(long silence)

Bill Bernbach: I have to go now. J Walter has got a couple of tickets to Johnny Cash and Buddy Holly's new band.

(silence)

Marie Beresford: He is fading....

Dave Bedwood: Ah, quickly, Bill! What is it like on the other side? What does it look like? What happens to you when you die? Do you get to play chess with Einstein? Are there animals in heaven? Is God a man? What was before the Big Bang? Is there life on other planets? Will the universe go on expanding? Will Dare go on expanding? Is—

Marie Beresford: He's gone....

(long pause)

Sam Ball: Is Colonel Sanders still with us?

Would the Last Person to Leave Please Turn Out the Enlightenment?
by Laura Jordan Bambach

So, how many advertising people does it take to change a light bulb? Or put another way, to bring a brand to life? Until relatively recently, the answer was simple: however many teams the creative director threw at it.

Creativity has always been about collaboration. In the case of advertising, it's usually the collaboration between an art director and a copywriter. Traditionally the hallowed pair would work in solitary confinement, protecting the ownership of their ideas from everyone bar the head honcho and praying that their ideas would be the ones to go before the clients, to win the pitches and go into production. That way of working served the industry pretty well until recently, but back then the communications landscape was a lot more predictable. Because traditional campaigns needed money and equipment, you could see the competition from a mile off. Digital channels and audiences have shaken up the industry, and things are starting to look radically different.

In the digital realm, we have a rapidly changing, ever-expanding list of deliverables, constantly in prototype and with the added intricacies of a medium that is more personal and an audience that is at once increasingly demanding and more-or-less able to manipulate and contribute to our output. But it's not just the medium that demands new ways of working; the people working in digital seem to demand it too. We are throwing ourselves into deeper collaborative processes within our own teams (or lack thereof), our clients, our consumers, and even with other agencies. With the growth of "media-neutral" briefs and integrated communication plans, this collaboration is lifting us out of the "digital ghetto" and is essential for survival.

WHERE DOES OUR DESIRE TO COLLABORATE COME FROM?

Why does collaboration come so easily to agencies that have grown from digital? Is it to do with it being a medium in its comparative infancy? Is it to do with how the "digital industry" has developed and the companies and individuals leading the way? Or is it just because the projects are bigger and more complicated, requiring a workforce able to change roles, software, and team structures at the drop of a hat?

In fact, it's all three, and it's a great success. That's why any "traditional" agencies worth their salt are looking to digital agencies as models for change. However, by the time they get there, digital roles will have changed again, as what we are asked to create takes another leap forward – not only into new delivery platforms, but into those that were until recently associated with old-school advertising. Lucky for us, not just embracing change, but actively encouraging it is our lifeblood.

ALL THE YOUNG PUNKS

Since they started popping up around fifteen years ago, and particularly since the dot-com crash of 2000, digital creative agencies have been the underdogs. Digital has been to "above-the-line" advertising as photography was to fine arts throughout most of the twentieth century:- a medium by and for the people, seen as overtly utilitarian and creatively poor, and lacking in grand advertising "auteurs." Instead, digital grew in the margins and was developed by innovators who were mostly young, self-taught, and ready to make do with DIY tools.

The digital pioneers got started through a shared passion for the new or for the technology, or for the excitement that interactivity provides – not for the money. That momentum has continued in no small part because of the crash. After all, who apart from a maverick would seek to work in an industry that's shutting down around them? It should be no surprise that their young, independent, and hungry agencies look and feel quite different from traditional companies and place a great emphasis on the social – on conversation and the discussion of ideas that comes from authentically shared attitudes.

There's no standard set of requirements for many of the positions available. We're still small enough as an industry to adapt to the rapidly changing advertising landscape, and we haven't found the perfect team structure yet. Maybe there isn't one, and that's the point.

So our industry is made up of people from a very broad base of multiple skills and experiences. We've matched a rich array of skills with a willingness to experiment, creating a myriad of agency set-ups and individual kinds of creative departments. People in digital feel that it's possible to do something that makes a difference. Their can-do attitude comes from having had to solve problems with less for so long. Most importantly, digital people are doers.

NECESSITY IS THE MOTHER OF COLLABORATION

By their nature, digital projects require a great deal of collaboration. Whether in-house or outsourced, the complex production processes involved can't be separated from the conceptual stage as cleanly as with older formats. The killer idea could just as easily be a technical solution as a traditional advertising concept. So digital innovators are interacting with one another in new ways, acting as suppliers and partners to get the job done and calling on one another's expertise and point of view.

Within digital agencies, collaboration is essential to the creative process. It enables us to select from a myriad of possible channels and techniques, from mobile to web to digital outdoor, and increasingly more traditional media, such as events and film or all of the above. A creative teams up with a "creative technologist" one day and an "experience architect" the next. Or perhaps one of the media planners. Or all of the above. Without deep collaboration, we can't ensure that our work is usable and accessible or successfully social. We can't be agile enough to take advantage of all the opportunities that rapidly changing technology affords us. Collaboration allows us to think big or small, move fast, and develop ideas that are truly integrated.

BEING TRANSPARENT

Embrace the tenet that collaboration doesn't mean compromise. Being precious and secretive about your ideas has no place in a truly collaborative environment, and working with the best possible people means that you won't need to compromise on the quality of the idea, even if that idea changes somewhat in the process. The ownership of the idea is shared, and all are better for it.

Bring everyone into the process, and don't be territorial. Pull in inspiration from all over the place. Choose your project team early, based on their skill set, and brief them together at the very beginning. Encourage the project team to work as a matrix of skills, not a hierarchy with the traditional creative team at the top. Creativity comes from diversity, so make sure that brainstorms are open to the entire project team and that the "creatives" can ask as many questions as possible. One of the most successful brainstorming techniques I've experienced was to bring in anyone in the company – even the receptionist – who had a particular affinity with the brand. The "creatives" then had a full arsenal of ideas at their disposal to dismiss or shape into whatever they desired, with the help of the rest of the team.

Encourage feedback on the ideas and make creative choices sooner, with the understanding and backing of the whole project team. Speak with your client and their consumers as often as you can. Good agencies understand that they make better products if they collaborate with their users earlier in the process.

Finally, be totally transparent with your client about your process and methodologies, particularly about outsourcing work. You can't really be collaborating if the client doesn't know about it. Blog about your work. Share your research and bookmarks, and get the client to contribute too. Rather than the comfortable way of doing things, with a front about how capable you are, show off your collaborative credentials. Explain that you're going to use third parties because they're the best of breed and the best equipped to do the work. The client doesn't have to manage these relationships, so be open and honest to them and maybe even bring the client closer to the project as well.

HE AIN'T HEAVY, HE'S MY BROTHER

Only very recently has "digital" shown up on the grand advertising radar as something that people should pay attention to. Perhaps it's even doing the unthinkable and becoming just a little glamorous. But in reality, a lot of us are just geeks and dreamers. Our agencies may all be different, but what we do have is camaraderie and a real sense of shared passion. And we love to collaborate with one another, even if we're also fierce competitors. In fact, when we *do* work together, we see one another more as partners than simply people providing a service.

Creative Social is one example: creative directors from the world's "best of breed" digital agencies regularly getting together to share ideas, unfinished work, inspiration, and vigorous debate. We also work together as a team to propel ourselves further into the broader advertising universe. The organisation SheSays is another example: a cross-agency organisation with a growing membership, where event topics and organisational growth come directly from the members themselves.

NEW KIDS ON THE BLOG

It was not by accident that the ideas of "open source" and "creative commons licensing" appeared first in the digital realm. Every home computer with an internet connection has the potential to be a content provider and media producer. As a consequence, brands themselves are increasingly becoming facilitators, rather than town criers – facilitators for over a billion end-users to collaborate, create, debate, comment, and share.

It's the antithesis of what advertising used to be all about and what Guy Debord imagined in *Society of the Spectacle,* where relationships between people are mediated by commodity and image, and where "passive identification with the spectacle supplants genuine activity." Instead, authenticity is paramount. Participation *is* the new spectacle, and that means digital agencies have had to develop fresh rules for collaboration with these newly empowered consumers. They are no longer a captive audience but now offer a sliding scale of authentic engagement and potential contributions and critique. We have had to let go of the creative reins and our sense of authorship in a way that runs contrary to how traditional agencies – and some clients – like to operate.

Offering a genuine opportunity for consumers to collaborate with you is a brave step, but letting them do so creates a sense of ownership and a desire to become part of a brand in a truly deep way. Want "word of mouth" to work for you? Deeply collaborate with your consumers, and you've got it.

WHAT MAKES A GOOD CREATIVE LEADER IN A COLLABORATIVE ENVIRONMENT?

Creativity grows best in the fertile ground of conversation. Just imagine...advertising has never been so much fun. Deep collaboration is often boisterous, energetic, and on the edge of chaos, so how do you get results out the other end? As the head of a digital creative department, your staff may include (but are not limited to):

- traditional creative teams (art director/copywriter)
- graphic designers
- flash developers
- front-end developers
- animators
- illustrators
- photographers
- motion graphics and postproduction
- lighting technicians
- storyboard artists
- information architects
- sound engineers
- experience architects
- creative technologists
- video editors
- ...and sometimes even planners

So what constitutes good creative leadership? An eye for detail? A great head for copy? The ability to spot a good idea? These traditional values are a good starting point, but effective creative leaders who embrace collaboration have a number of other common traits that make them successful:

- Be reachable, be conversational, be transparent. Listen as well as talk. Have conversations with your staff and remember them. Deep collaboration relies on those involved feeling comfortable about expressing their ideas in front of you and on you being able to steer the team in the right direction with universal buy-in.
- Be open to good ideas coming from anywhere.
- Be able to put together the best team for the job. Know people's strengths and play to them. Pair people with mentors so that every project is a learning experience.
- Be clear about the project boundaries. Provide a clear and compelling sense of purpose to help engage the team's collective imaginations. Lay out some simple rules, and let the team manage itself, rather than telling them what to do.
- I once heard someone say that imagination without memory is like building bricks out of papier mâché. As a creative leader, your job is to be the collective memory for the project. What has happened in previous projects? What obstacles do we need to look out for? Why did it work so well last time? In an open forum, you need these reference points to come to quick, beneficial decisions.
- Be a good facilitator who can enable others to keep a project focused and under control.
- Fight for the time in project preparation for your team to absorb. Everyone involved needs to assimilate the idea for it to stay on track.
- Spot and enable another good leader. Good leadership in a collaborative atmosphere relies on leadership at many levels, not just from the top down. Don't be afraid of

resting responsibility on other people's shoulders and empowering them to take control.

- Be a motivator. Invest in social capital. Be inspirational, and constantly funnel inspiration to your teams from as many sources as possible. Attract interesting people to join you.
- Say thank you. Set clear incentives and rewards.

Leading innovation and creativity is often like leading a creative conversation. That is why open and collaborative ways of working demand new open and collaborative approaches to leadership.

YOU ARE WHAT YOU EAT

In digital-centered agencies, hierarchies aren't as steep, department boundaries are more porous, and job descriptions are more open. Teams are modular and skills-based. Deep collaboration takes place within our walls, with our clients, with our consumers, and with one another.

Employees increasingly need to be flexible, self-motivated problem solvers, not rigid rule followers. More jobs will involve the investment of imagination, creativity, and empathy – factors of production that are difficult to measure. People will be expected to multitask and deliver and execute effectively, but also to innovate and learn. A performance-based pay system that rewards individual efforts and output will do little to encourage new ideas and collaboration.

We are in a good space. But even those bigger, older, and more traditional advertising agencies are learning from the way we work so that they can remain effective. The clever ones are already embracing it. They are becoming more democratic, open, and egalitarian to match the innovation capacity of "digital." Perhaps when these changes are more widespread we really will have no such thing as a digital agency anymore. But for the moment, regardless of the work we're producing, our digital heritage and its collaborative mindset will still set us apart. The most important question for us now is, where to next?

How Advertising Can Become a Friend Whose Company You Enjoy, Rather Than Just an Annoying Salesman Who Sticks His Foot in the Door
by Sam de Volder

My family and I go to Ikea every now and again, just like everyone else. And just like everyone else, if we end up there around lunchtime, it's not uncommon for us to succumb to those incredibly delicious meatballs. Things usually proceed according to a set pattern. My three kids run like crazy to the play corner where they put on a show for Mum (whose primary concern, of course, is the safety of the other children). Dad, however, goes on ahead to order and stand in line, arranging everything as elegantly as possible on three trays and sliding up to the cashier.

In most self-service cafeterias, I would now face a difficult decision: do I carry the trays to the starving lions one at a time, or like some kind of circus act, do I attempt to stack two trays on top of each other, thus saving one trip with an overloaded tray? (Note that the play corner is usually located in the furthest corner of the restaurant.) Or better still: do I take a risk, call my eldest son (eight), stick a tray between his fingers, and lose two years off my life watching him joyfully carve a swerving path through a sea of tables, chairs, and people? Hmm, a tough nut to crack – all the more so with an ever-impatient queue of people gathering behind me.

But not so at Ikea. A special trolley allows you to insert three trays neatly on top of one another, effortlessly wheel them over to your table, and start devouring those delicious meatballs in no time at all – completely stress-free. I thought that was great: a brand that really thinks from the standpoint of the consumer and does everything to make his life easier and better, without being asked. And it works. My respect for Ikea is even greater as a result. That's when I thought: wouldn't it be great if every brand was like that? Including and especially when it comes to advertising.

We have to accept that advertising was for a long time (and often still is) about how to trick consumers into buying a product – not to mention brainwashing them. But something has changed. Partly thanks to interactive media, consumers have become more vocal and are no longer so easily walked over. It's also easier in this digital age to avoid advertising. You press a couple of buttons, and hey presto, you skip the ads. That's an inconvenient truth as well, for let's be honest: people view advertising as a necessary evil. (Heck, a lot of people probably don't even see what's so necessary about it, even though in many cases it's advertising that ensures we can see our favourite series on TV, read our newspaper, or go to the football.) There are, in other words, black clouds on the horizon in advertising land.

If there is one major difference between traditional and digital advertising, it is that, in digital, the consumer has to make the first move. He or she has to click something or fill in an address to come and see for him or herself. So what the consumer gets to see actually needs to be worth that initial effort – doubly so if it's advertising. Because if you make an effort as a consumer and come away disappointed, the chances are slim that people will listen the next time the same brand has something to say. That's not rocket science. The major challenge is to make people appreciate advertising. And that is possible. You can, for instance, ensure that the message is entertaining or perhaps socially responsible, advertising that makes the world a better place (both of these concepts are explored elsewhere in this book).

You can also make sure your advertising is useful. Huh? Useful? That might sound like the knitted beanies and mittens Grandma used to give you for Christmas. It doesn't have to be like that. Useful is good. It means that people can do something with it.

Wouldn't it be fantastic as a brand to make advertising that not only sells your product but also helps people get more out of their lives? Your audience would then feel that the brand really understands them, that it goes to the trouble of getting more out of the original product or service. In such cases, consumers repay the gesture with their respect and gratitude –priceless things that are getting hard to buy outright these days. *Branded utility* – to use a buzzword – has less to do with humorous clips or funny stories but is a terrain where brands can really forge links with their consumers because it's clear that there's something in it for them.

How do you go about that as a brand? First and foremost, look at what your brand promise is, something you no doubt (passively) announced to your customers years ago. And then look at how you can help your target group to realise that brand promise effectively.

That is the case with the branded utility example *par excellence*: Nike+ by Nike and Apple. Put simply, you have a chip in your shoe that transmits information about your run to your iPod (where while you run you get encouragement from, among others, the likes of Lance Armstrong). You can then link your iPod to the Nike+ site and keep track of how you do. You can also share your experience with joggers from all over the world, form groups, challenge one another, compare performances.... The whole set-up has been designed to stimulate and motivate you to run better and harder, or in my case, to finally forget the excuses and get my fat arse on the road. Nike+ is the friend that runs with you. It is the coach that motivates you. It is the pat on the back that encourages you to do better and keep it going. Nike+ is thus a fantastic example of how brands can go a step further in actually keeping their brand promise. It is the difference between preaching "Just do it" and taking the opportunity and the responsibility to get people running and to motivate and stimulate them to improve. Of course, we shouldn't be too naive here. For Nike and Apple, of course, it is still about innovation and in the end, product sales. But that makes the story all the more beautiful because everyone wins here: the two brands, the jogger, and also the community that helps one another.

This is also a great example of how the boundaries can blur between the product, a service, advertising, and community building. Take one of the elements away, and the whole thing collapses like a house of cards. Ingenious, smart, and useful!

Another approach is to look at what needs are out there in society and more specifically among consumers. Then look at how your brand or product can forge a link.

Do you want to lead an active life? Great, because that is just what Stadium, a sports store chain, wants as well. And to help they compiled a map of unique jogging routes for thirty-three Swedish cities as part of the campaign "The City Is Your Stadium." Beyond the fact that it's nice as a jogger to get to know a different route every now and again, Stadium also marked a number of places in the city where you can get even more out of your workout. Park benches suddenly became stretch planks; escalators, places to work on your quads. Stadium even included clothing advice for the weather condition at that exact moment and, of course, the locations of Stadium stores in the neighbourhood. This is an intelligent example of how a brand message ("live an active life") is intertwined with a concrete sales push (the outfits) and a store locator (shops on the route) in a package that's really useful to you as a jogger (the jogging route and the exercises).

Another strong example is the "NonstopFernando" campaign by the airline Emirates. Emirates wanted to announce that you can now fly from Dubai to São Paolo in just fourteen hours and forty minutes (it used to take a lot longer). To bring attention to this fact, they made a film in which a guy named Fernando talks about how fantastic São Paolo is for fourteen hours and forty minutes. He talks about the beach, the girls, the flip-flops, the clubs, the cocktails, the food, the places to be, the football, and so on. The film is available not only on the internet, but also on one of the in-flight entertainment channels on the plane. Fernando gives you a crash course in São Paolo so you can experience the city as he does – like a local in the know. And he doesn't just talk about it in the film. You can look up Fernando on Delicious, the website where visitors share their favourite links, and immediately click through to sites offering extra information on the topics he discusses in the film. If he's talking about a certain restaurant, for example, you can click through to the restaurant's own website, peruse the menu, check the opening hours, and look up the address. On Fernando's Last.fm page, you can also listen to music by the musicians he talks about. What better way to get into the groove for your trip to São Paolo? Convenient and useful. Best of all, you're constantly reminded that, with Emirates, you can now get to your destination a whole lot quicker than before.

As you can see, branded utility can be the basis for a product (such as Nike+) and it can be a campaign (such as Stadium or Emirates). However, it can also be simple tools and applications that offer added value for consumers while still pushing a brand clearly to the fore.

Take H&M, for example. Now, I like to be well dressed, but I'm hopeless at matching clothes and really don't have the time to run around the shops. H&M came to the rescue with their virtual fitting room. I can mix and match all I want online, and then all I have to do in the shop is grab the right size. That's it. Hassle-free.

Another approach is to offer content, for example, in the form of downloads. Thanks to the omnipresence these days of MP3 players, people are always looking for cool content to liven up their iPod or other player – hence, the incredible surge of audiobooks over the past few years. In this sense, it was terribly clever of BMW to commission a few wild, exhilarating stories by established authors (in which the only reference to BMW was that the leading characters every so often, with relative subtlety, get into a BMW to drive through their adventures). Those stories were then offered as free audiobooks by BMW. For fans of podcasts and audiobooks (and there are a lot of them), it's a great gesture that has increased appreciation for the brand considerably.

Usefulness will also play a big role in the further appreciation of mobile apps. Just think of a way your brand (promise) or product can be of use when people are on the go – or need to go, like Charmin, a P&G-owned toilet paper brand showed. When you're in the city, public restrooms can offer a horrifying, nearly traumatic experience. But not with the mobile application called SitOrSquat that Charmin decided to sponsor. SitOrSquat is a GPS-based mobile application that tells you where the nearest restrooms are located and more important – thanks to user reviews – how clean they are. I admit, it would have been even nicer if Charmin had invented the application themselves (sitorsquat.com has existed since 2007), but still this sponsorship and turning it into a mobile application is simple and easy and just smart marketing (a consumer in need probably couldn't care less anyway).

Usefulness will also play a big role in social media. First consider the nature and specifics of the social network. Then see if you can add something that enhances the experience of its users, not forgetting the relevance for your brand or message. A great example: we know that people who travel a lot like to share where they are. Lufthansa, therefore, launched an application called MySkyStatus that shares your flight status while airborne via Twitter or Facebook. On the one hand, it's a status-enhancing application; on the other hand, it can also be useful for your colleagues, friends, or partner to know on the spot where you are, if your flight is delayed or on time, and so on. For Lufthansa, every single tweet or post on Facebook offers free publicity. The great thing about MySkyStatus is that it's open to all airlines – a bold and brave approach for Lufthansa and the right thing to do, as it facilitated a better and faster adoption of the application.

Whatever you do, the strongest examples are those that succeed in not only helping to satisfy a need but also succeeding in making the initiative relevant for the brand. It's important that people see the link between what you offer them and the product or brand. Ideally, the initiative should be completely interwoven with the product or brand so that the end result is something unique that fits only that brand.

In striving for this outcome, it's a great advantage to think as early as possible about how a product is best launched onto the market. As is discussed elsewhere in this book, in the coming years agencies will strive to be involved much earlier in the picture and in certain cases even participate in the product development process itself (as opposed to in the past where a product was simply plonked on the table and then off to work you went). The streamlined approach of Nike+ demonstrates that a total experience can bear a lot of fruit: a brilliant product, smart advertising, and a satisfied consumer.

Another terrific example of a seamless collaboration between a brand and its agency is Fiat eco:Drive. By now we are all aware of our ecological footprints, but acting upon that knowledge is often easier said than done. You can use your car less, but how can you change your driving style for the better? For those who are willing to act and change the way they drive, Fiat eco:Drive offers a solution. The car is equipped with software that tracks your driving behaviour. Everything is stored on a USB stick that you plug into your computer. Then a user-friendly desktop application called eco:Drive analyses your real and accurate journey data. The results allow Fiat drivers to easily understand how they can improve their driving techniques and habits to reduce CO_2 emissions and save money on fuel. Over 4 million journeys have been logged and analysed. The application is connected to a community called eco:Ville, where Fiat drivers can connect and share experiences and insights. For Fiat, eco:Drive and eco:Ville will probably prove to become great platforms that allow ongoing conversations with customers in the coming years.

However things may develop from here on out, it's clear that branded utility will only become more important in years to come because it's one of the best ways to make advertising really relevant and interesting for the consumer. It helps advertising become a friend whose company you really enjoy, rather than just an annoying salesperson who sticks his or her foot in the door. If you ever doubt which path you should take with your campaign, just pause a minute to consider those meatballs at Ikea. Works for me.

Why Don't You Just Switch Off Your Television Set and Go and Do Something Less Boring Instead?
by Jon Sharpe

Scary, isn't it – the tyranny of the blank page? So what did you do with it? Doodle? Make copious notes on the eloquent musings of my co-contributors? Finally make a start on that novel? Redesign the ceiling of the Sistine Chapel? Get hold of some animal faeces and plaster them all over it in a deeply ironic pastiche of Chris Ofili?

Nothing?! What do you mean you did nothing? But you're "The User," aren't you? You're that guy that everyone, and I mean everyone, keeps talking about. You even scooped *Time Magazine*'s Person of the Year in 2006, didn't you? You're a creative genius, a maverick, a rebel without a cause, the future of the internet – aren't you? You're amazing! You're like Rupert Murdoch, Samuel Pepys, Johann Sebastian Bach, Mario Testino, and Banksy all rolled into one, right? Oh, and didn't I hear you were obscenely good-looking and great in the sack to boot?

Well, whilst you're deliberating which aspect of your multifaceted genius to lay down, let me take you on a little trip down memory lane. In the UK in the 1970s, we had three television channels, two of which were firmly occupied by our much-lauded public sector broadcaster, the BBC. On weekday mornings during the school holidays, BBC1 ran a show called *Why Don't You?* that in some senses could be viewed as an early precursor to the contemporary BBC's wholehearted embrace of user-generated content (UGC). The show featured groups of pallid schoolchildren chorusing the refrain "Why don't you just switch off your television set and go and do something less boring instead?" in largely unintelligible regional accents. They would then implore us to experience such thrills as, er, cutting some paper into shapes or learning a rudimentary magic trick. We didn't bother, of course. We couldn't be arsed. We did nothing, beyond watching yet more TV, as was our wont. But somehow that was the point. If we had actually gone off and "done something less boring instead," then the show wouldn't have had an audience. And audiences were what TV producers got paid for.

In his speech "Gin, Television, and Social Surplus,"[1] Clay Shirky argues that the critical technology of the twentieth century was TV. It was TV that allowed us to absorb the shock of the huge postwar growth in free time, in much the same way that gin was the critical technology that enabled us to manage the shock of transition from rural life to urban life during the Industrial Revolution of the nineteenth century. Shirky goes on to suggest that it's only recently that we've begun to see the resulting "cognitive surplus" – created by rising GDP per capita, rising educational attainment, rising life expectancy, and a rising number of people working five-day work weeks – as an asset rather than a crisis. Consequently, we've started to deploy it in ways more interesting than simply staring at the TV.

---

[1] Clay Shirky, "Gin, Television, and Social Surplus"
<http://www.herecomeseverybody.org/2008/04/looking-for-the-mouse.html>

Fascinating though Shirky's argument is, endemic to it is a presumption that that there was a time BC (before creativity) when we were mindless automata that consumed but didn't create, and a time AC (after creativity) when our collective muse suddenly hit and we were all simultaneously overcome by an egalitarian desire to share. But that simply isn't the case. People creating stuff is nothing new. It's just that back in the day when we weren't watching *Why Don't You?* blogs were called *diaries,* playlists were called *mix tapes,* and photostreams were called *photo albums.* Performance Artist Laurie Anderson once said that "technology is the campfire around which we tell our stories," suggesting that, although technology may be the enabler, the fundamental need both to create and share is as old as humankind itself.

Furthermore, brands (in particular media brands) have always solicited content. From the righteous (newspaper Letters to the Editor) to the reactionary (Points of View–style feedback shows on TV and radio), to the comedic (home video bloopers) and the illicit (graffiti and remixing), UGC has been a feature of the media landscape for decades. Until recently, though, it was predominantly the province of the outraged, the disenfranchised, the politicized, or those prone to exhibitionism. The rest of us just went back to our diaries, mix tapes, and photographs. Or, if we were really stuck for something to do, we went back to watching *Why Don't You?*

So what changed? From YouTube to the blogosphere, from Facebook to peer reviews, there has been a veritable Cambrian explosion of UGC of late. But what's been the catalyst behind the deluge? As far as I can tell, it's due to two key factors.

1. The Means of Distribution

    The first factor lies in the means of distribution – that is, in the days of *Why Don't You?* we didn't really have one. Our audience was either extremely limited – a bored sibling, a distracted parent, or even a slightly bemused pet – or was nonexistent. But the internet has dealt with that little problem, as it has with so many others, and The Long Tail means that, at least potentially, all of us now have an audience.

This is key, for as much as we may respect the artist who solipsistically toils to no avail towards a lonely end, most of us harbour a prejudice that a comedian is truly a comedian only if people laugh, a writer if people read, a musician if people listen, a photographer if people look. We feel that audiences can exist without content but that content isn't really content without an audience. Audiences motivate us to create, and their feedback motivates us to continue to do so.

Our innate desire to exploit these potential audiences has been further fuelled by the rapidly dwindling price of technology. Software such as GarageBand or iMovie, which are now bundled free with any purchase of an Apple Mac, would have cost tens of thousands of pounds to purchase only ten years ago. This shift has allowed us to create media of a standard that hitherto has been firmly the preserve of professionals. Of course, the means to create quality and the ability to actually do so are two very different things, but however deviant our stuff may be, we can bet that there will be someone, somewhere who will dig it. The instantaneous and economical means of distribution that the internet provides gives us all the opportunity to find or, more likely, be discovered by, a likeminded and appreciative audience. Humans need positive reinforcement, whether that's around the campfire or anywhere else. We seek praise with pitiful certainty, and the anonymity that the internet provides gives us a useful hedge against public humiliation. The combination is beguiling, and together with the ease of publication, it is the first factor to have informed the recent unabated surge in UGC.

2. The Absence of Authority

As discussed previously, brands (in particular media brands) soliciting stuff is nothing new. The problem was that what these brands wanted us to create and what we wanted to create were, more often than not, two different things. These brands would solicit and display content only on their own terms, according to their own agendas, and within their own strict protocols. In order to be published, we had to kowtow. But that has changed, and the BBC's metamorphosis since the days of three television channels and *Why Don't You?* is instructive. For the world's oldest public sector broadcaster, steeped in the culture of devolving content created by the privileged few to the many, to allow anyone to edit, co-create, and demand content represents a massive cultural shift and is one that many other brands would do well to heed. Witnessing the steady conversion of its viewers, readers, and listeners into users, authors, and contributors, the BBC was faced with little choice and to stem a dwindling audience share, rapidly applied the age-old principle of "if you can't beat 'em, join 'em."

It is this usurping of the authoritative editor by the masses and the emergence of The Wisdom of Crowds, James Surowiecki's concept that groups, through the aggregation of information, often make better decisions than could have been made by any single member of the group, that is the second factor that has informed the exponential rise of UGC. This one has firmly underpinned some of its most notorious success stories, such as Wikipedia.

So, presented with this new paradigm, what should brands do? And what should agencies do? And, perhaps most importantly, what the hell should you, "The User," do?

Well, if you're a brand, the answer is surprisingly simple: ask not what your consumers can do for you, but what you can do for your consumers. Treat your consumers as collaborators. Facilitate, don't legislate. And be honest, truthful, and sincere. The rise of the peer review means that anything disingenuous will be found out and then amplified. You can find many instructive examples of this new mode of brand behaviour to seek inspiration from.

Nike, for instance, behaves like an events company (RunLondon) one minute, a bespoke tailor the next (Nike ID), and a software developer the next (Nike+), providing different points of access for different consumers but always allowing those consumers to play the role of protagonist. But this approach isn't limited to so-called "cool brands." Brands such as Boeing, Lego and Doritos are all getting in on the act by variously inviting their consumers to collaborate on the design of new aeroplanes, create and sell their own toys, and even create content for some of the most expensive advertising spots in history. The user-generated ads featured in the Doritos 2010 "Crash the Super Bowl" campaign not only delighted its vast TV audience but also resulted in an astonishing 18 million online views in the week immediately following the big game – a testament to the merits of harnessing UGC if ever there was one.

And what of agencies? Jay Chiat, the founder of Chiat\Day, once famously said that "creative is not a department." And he was right. But neither is creative an advertising agency. So aside from breaking the monopoly that traditional art director–copywriter creative teams typically exercise over the creative process, agencies also need to look beyond their environs and, like brands, begin to treat consumers as collaborators. We live in a beta culture where consumers actively want to liaise with you as you develop content and will happily bear with you as you seek to improve it. Your audience is no longer captive, and their relationship with media is evolving faster than ever. So it's vital that you involve them, consult with them, and listen to them – well before the focus group.

So finally back to you, "The User." Have you actually created anything yet? Or are you still just consuming this? Don't you know that consuming is just sooooooooo 2005? Well, whilst you're thinking about what to do with those blank pages in between filming yourself singing in the shower, updating your social networking status, doing your citizen journalist bit, editing that scurrilous entry about you on Wikipedia, and perfecting your Dolly Parton-meets-Megadeth mash-up, can I make a suggestion? Your name stinks. It's awful. "The User" is a derogatory and divisive term, more redolent of drug addicts and confidence tricksters than of a valued creative voice. It also infers a nonsensical distinction between them and us, the haves and the have-nots, the mass media publisher and the individual publisher, which is wholly erroneous when it comes to matters of quality and integrity. So why not stop being "The User"? Change your name, but not your deeds, for with UGC comes a noble purpose: democracy. It levels the media playing field and offers opportunity to those who really want it, rather than simply those who inherited it. So embrace it. Be a Publisher, an Artist, a Journalist, a Developer, a Musician, a Photographer, an Agitator, a Prosumer, or an Agent Provocateur. Be all of the above. Just don't be "The User." "The User" is what they define you as, whoever they may be. Elude definition.

Sound in Digital Advertising
by Rafa Soto

We learn to hear before we are born. Hearing is the first sense we develop – and one of the first we use to relate with the world – which makes sound one of the most powerful tools for generating emotions.

In advertising, sound is responsible, in most cases, for supplying the general emotional layer of an ad. Remove the sound layer from any ad you can think of, and it loses its essential quality.

Thus, in advertising, music is the creator and accelerator of emotions. We have to create a specific atmosphere in a short time, and a few musical notes or sound effects will tell you quicker than anything whether it is humour, horror, action, surrealism, or love.

And if sound is crucial in ads, it is even more so in digital advertising: firstly, because when somebody is browsing the internet they usually do so with dozens of windows and applications open at the same time, and we want them to concentrate solely on ours. Secondly, a laptop or desktop screen in an office cannot compare to a cinema screen with Dolby

Surround. If we wish to transmit an emotion, we have to make a much greater effort.

Let us imagine, for example, a reel of images by a landscape photographer – first without music and then with evocative music that succeeds in carrying you off to that place. A clear example can be found at the website for the art exhibition 'Ashes and Snow' (www.ashesandsnow.org), where the music noticeably enhances the content of the photos.

And while we are thinking of music as an evocative element in interactive experiences, I can think of no better examples than almost all the pieces at Orisinal (www.orisinal.com), a website featuring 60 Adobe Flash games. They are already classics but have withstood the test of time unscathed; they are still up to date thanks, in large part, to the sound. In spite of their simplicity, I believe that these games are a fine example of how to transmit emotions online through good use of sound. Another excellent example is the game that unit9 created for Honda - www.unit9.com/grrrgame – very simple, with an isometric perspective, and with no great effort made in the production, but the music makes it magical.

At Herraiz & Soto, we once made a piece for BMW (www.bmw.es/microsites/motores_s5/microsite/) where, although everything was highly minimalistic, the sound intensified the experience greatly. In this case, we generated the sound randomly using different scales on the piano, but the result is still extremely moving and thanks to the experience, time spent on the microsite increased by 400 per cent, and 75 per cent of the users interacted with the whole piece.

But besides the music and special effects, the sound in any digital production is crucial for obtaining good feedback. The most intense way of transmitting the sensation of touch is through sound; it can convey the texture, the intensity, and all the nuances of what we are touching.

The sound on screen virtually substitutes the sense of touch, and by working with good textures, it is possible to achieve truly incredible atmospheres – something which, thanks to the use of sound and interactivity, cannot be obtained with audiovisual ads. There is a game/experience that explains this well: flow (http://intihuatani.usc.edu/cloud/flowing), produced by That Game Company. This is a minimalistic game in which you simply have to evolve. The project has won prizes worldwide thanks to its capacity for transmitting emotions, and the sound is one of the responsible factors.

Another great example where sound substitutes very well for touch is Theturn.tv (www.theturn.tv) - an experimental website for a music band, Fredo Viola, that will make you feel the elements as if you were really playing with them. But not just that – interactivity + sound = musical instrument. No doubt many of you have spent some time exploring the possibilities of musical instruments. Just playing them to find out how they sound. And no doubt many of you have had tremendous experiences with no narrative sense, but which nevertheless have been highly intense.

One simple experiment by the artist Sébastien Chevrel (www.seb.cc/spacializer) may serve to explain, in a simple and inspirational way, what can be obtained with just music. Other good examples include www.pianographique.com, a site which allows you to compose your own music with your keyboard while you create graphic designs on your monitor and the Mercedes C-Class site (www.c-class.co.uk), a site which allows you to explore the features of the car through a combination of abstract images and sound.

Nevertheless, one of the best pieces that I have come across in this sense was not on the internet but on a Nintendo DS. Toshio Iwai's Electroplankton game is an absolute delight – probably the most successful piece in creatively uniting sound and interactivity to date (demo on YouTube: www.youtube.com/watch?v=N10XSF63VY4).

Another of the most emotive interactive experiences with sound produced to date is *Messa di Voce* (www.tmema.org/messa), by Golan Levin and Zach Lieberman, an interactive experience in which sound acquires form and interacts with the user. This pure sensation of viewing and playing with sound is an area that has been explored much less than the purely audiovisual one, and it is full of possibilities.

And talking about installations, programmers and musicians are creating new visual devices to play music in a more intuitive manner. I'm sure this is only the beginning, but it is currently a powerful source of inspiration if you're thinking about creating an installation for one of your interactive projects. One of them is Reactable (www.reactable.com/reactable/), a project born in Barcelona consisting of an interactive table that reads different objects that you place on the surface. Another is called Tenori-On (www.global.yamaha.com/design/tenori-on/swf/index.html), created by Toshio Iwai. It's an extremely simple tablet that allows you to create beautiful compositions in a very easy way.

Incidentally, in Japan small undulations have been built into a number of roads so that when cars pass over them they produce melodies. Thus, in the hands of creativity, there is still a long way to go for music and interactivity.

But working with sound is not only about creating music or effects to make graphics bolder; it can also work the other way round. We recently created an experience for the band Labuat that used graphics to provide an even deeper relationship with the music. The concept (http://soytuaire.labuat.com/) was simple: we created an intelligent brush that was listening, beating, and reacting to the music and the lyrics in real time, allowing the user to quite literally "paint a song." Another simple but strong idea is the website for the band FPM (www.fpmnet.com), created by Yugo Nakamura that makes the fonts react to the music in very elegant and different ways.

Anyway I truly believe that sounds are still heavily underutilized online, and I look forward to seeing an increased use in the future. If you are interested in using sound more, here are a few basic tips for effective sound production:

- **Spend time on sound.** The most normal thing is to leave the sound part until the end. If you think of the audio as a key creative element, productions will gain in quality all round.

- **Use good effects.** Very often I see work in which there has been a lot of investment in photography or illustration, but the sound is really weak. If you want something that is high quality, the sound must be high quality; this is often not the case with free effects on the internet.
- **Design original sounds.** Just as in art management, you can copy or you can start from scratch with a distinctive personality. In 1985 Koji Kondo created a unique sound for Super Mario, which is still being used today.
- **Dispense with loops.** If you use musical loops, at least make them very long. The best thing is to generate melodies based on mutually compatible musical scales.
- **Work with professionals.** In the same way that a photographer will take a better photo, a musician's experience is vital if you want to produce a high-quality proposal.
- **Be subtle.** Silence is the equivalent of blank space in art management. If there are too many elements, you simply can't see the woods for the trees. The same is true for sound.

The Latin Spirit
by Fernanda Romano

Since the Cannes Cyber Lions were first spawned, my native country Brazil has fared phenomenally well. As a result of this, the top advertising agencies in London, New York, and San Francisco are littered with Brazilians. What is it that makes Latin Americans so creative? Is it the culture? The weather? The food?

I don't think the answer lies entirely in genetics, although I'd like to believe I could blame it on "the melting pot," which is a fantastic concept to explain the way we live, how we look, and why is it that the best sushi in the world can be found in São Paulo (in case you don't know, Brasil has the largest community of Japanese outside of Japan). I also don't believe we (the Latin Americans, I mean) are a separate people with some sort of special ability to add that "Latin flair" everyone talks about. Which brings me to what could be the real reason for the talent and the creative excellence you find in Latin America: bananas. Bananas have a lot of Vitamin B6, which is good for your brain. They have been associated with better memory, helping hangovers, and treating depression, because a banana helps metabolize tryptophan to serotonin. And that makes you happy. Happy people make for more creative people.

And then there's the sun. The sun helps you metabolize Vitamin D, which in turn strengthens the immune system and helps prevent several cancers and other illnesses. The sun is also responsible for better results in stock markets. According to research conducted by Dr. David Hirshleifer of the Ohio State University's Fisher College of Business, and Dr. Tyler Shumway, assistant professor of finance at the University of Michigan, on twenty-six leading global stock exchanges over a period of fifteen years, the results were better when there was sunshine. Many psychologists state that the sun's effect is good for your mood overall. Sunshine makes people feel happy, which makes them optimistic, and that can probably be connected to risk taking... and that can be traced to better and fresher ideas. Happy people make for more creative people.

But what about the heat? Heat can make you irritable. It can also make you tired. It certainly makes you want to be outside. Yes, OK, some people prefer to be inside with air conditioning – I know that. But I'm not talking about those people. Anyway, being outside is great. Add fresh air to enjoying the sun and spending time with other people. Ice-cold beer with friends. Time off. It resets the brain. It's very good for you. And let's not forget açai. This is the Brazilians' little secret, though I must admit I find it too sour. An antioxidant that is said to increase energy, açai is good for your heart and good for bodybuilding – yes, we don't really think of bodybuilders as smart people, but there is a governor in the States who might prove us wrong. And one doesn't have to be a bodybuilder to eat açai.

I guess when the Argentines read this they will say I made it way too Brazilian. I apologize for that. I do think many of the reasons listed refer to Argentines, Chileans, Peruvians, Mexicans, Costa Ricans, and Uruguayans as well. Official apologies to all the other countries I have not mentioned here. You are most certainly as creative as everybody else.

Going back to my point. Maybe it's not bananas, although I will maintain my sunshine theory. So, what is it that Latin Americans have that makes their work so interesting? I believe we are the right and wrong people in the right and wrong places. And that makes for a perfect storm of creativity. Here you go.

First fact: in Latin America the budgets are smaller. Think about MacGyver. When all you have to escape a prison – or solve a brief – is a toothbrush, a piece of chewing gum, and a tube of lipstick, you have to be creative.

Allow me to make an exception here for Argentina. Their budgets are not always that small. Due to the country's economic history and the very serious crisis between 1999 and 2002, many of the agencies have looked beyond their borders and started working with international clients on global campaigns. So now they have budgets like the Americans or the Brits have when they're producing their work. To be fair, the Argentines didn't become smarter then and suddenly start doing good work. They have a history and culture of good work. It just got better. And the truth is that they are still mostly focused on TV.

But we were talking about budgets. Limitation. Necessity is the mother of creativity. If you can't do a big show, your show must be better. You work harder. You study more.

Which brings me to a second fact: we are curious and shamelessly ignorant. We always look beyond our world to find inspiration: what is out there and who is doing great? This is the root of great creativity for Latin America, whether expressed through music, literature, architecture, or cuisine. We are a younger culture. We don't have much of a past or tradition. We don't have a way to do things. If one says "the British way," you can conjure an image in your mind's eye. Same goes for "the French way" or "the Japanese way." But the Brazilian way? *Jeitinho*, commonly known as what you come up with to escape an uncomfortable situation or to create an opportunity (usually to do something many people wouldn't call very proper). And this culture of looking for a better, more compelling argument, with less fuss (making do with what you have at your disposal) gave the creative community in these countries a lot of discipline to look for the best possible storytelling, be detail oriented, and master the visual arts.

Third fact: we are a mix of people. In an interview with *Boards* magazine[2], my old boss, Sergio Valente of DM9DDB said this about Brazilian advertising: "We are a multiracial society, more tolerant than some, more friendly than many. We do not have religion problems, racial problems, democracy problems. Our key problem is wealth distribution. But even in the extremes of society, one can find this lightness, this positiveness, this adaptability, this sureness that, by the end, everything is going to be all right. That is a very strong trait in our DNA." He went on to say that "one of the best aspects of Brazilian society, which is reflected in Brazilian advertising, is that we are not a self-centered culture, perhaps a result of these multiracial roots we have. We are open to the world, able to absorb the best the world has to give without losing our identity."

I'd like to say that this is a trait you see in advertising all over Latin America. Good advertising, of course. Strong and powerful inspiration coming from other places, seasoned with the sense of humor and the "air" of this Latin spirit.

Now, there are several consumer-related factors for why Brazil, for instance, does so well with its work for digital. Brazilians are early adopters of technology. The internet has higher penetration than paid TV, and among youth it is the media with the most affinity. I could go on. But the reason digital advertising in Brazil is good is simple: some incredibly talented and hard- working people inspired the digital creatives. And these guys had the opportunity, the technology, and the education (creatives usually come from wealthier families and are therefore well travelled and usually able to speak enough English to truly consume the world's culture). And they set the bar way too high. It is a culture that loves advertising. When you love what you do,

---

[2] Is there a Brazilian style? By Jonathan Link, Boards Magazine, October 1, 2006

you do it happily and happy people make for more creative people.

You see? I tried to be reasonable. I tried to look at genes. I tried to look at economic factors. However, none of them explain satisfactorily why every time someone thinks of advertising in Latin America, they wonder if it's something we put in the water. It is not. It is love. We are passionate. This mix of Portuguese, Spanish, English, Italian, African, Indian, Lebanese, Japanese, German, and who knows how many other cultures that make for our people – did you know there is a coastal town three hours south of Buenos Aires where nearly everybody is tall, red haired, and freckled? And the streets have weird names with loads of "ll" and "y." It was a Gaelic community. Just as in Brazil, there is still a city where most people speak German. But this is not the point, although I do believe the more diverse the cultural environment the richer and fresher and certainly more creative it can be. Ask Mark Waites at Mother London. He'll tell you.

Anyway, the point is that this mix made for some very passionate people. We don't like our advertising; we love it. And when you love what you do, you do it a lot. When you do it a lot, you do more of it. When you do more of it, statistically, you are bound to get some of it right. If it's a lot (a bit of a lot is a lot more than a bit of some) right, then some will be great. And if some is great, you will be very happy about it. And if you are happy about it, you will continue to do it. With love. This is the spirit. The Latin flair.

And, yes, it does help that we are all young economies – growing and competitive – and that even if we are not "the land of opportunity," we are people who chase an opportunity. So *good* is the real enemy of *excellent*, and we don't rest until we get there. We are really hard workers (as a note, I am rewriting this article on a Wednesday evening, a little after ten, and I just finished a presentation. I work in London. I am the only person here. Ah, here's the cleaning crew. They are Brazilians.)

It also helps that we celebrate our ad folks in a way few cultures do. In that I think the English and the Americans (in the sixties) are like us. Washington Olivetto, Marcello Serpa, Nizan Guanaes, Fernando Vega Olmos, Hernan Ponce. When we "grow up" we all want to be as successful as they are, and we will work like crazy until we get there. And of course you can always blame it on the fact that because we make pretty good money – at least in Brazil – our creatives rarely defect. They just work harder – to make more money.

About the bananas. I was never a great fan of bananas. They are nice snacks. Better than cereal bars, anyway. Of course, in Brazil they taste much better than in the US or in Europe, though in Spain they are all right. Probably imported, though. I was just thinking that maybe the bananas are really to blame for some of it. Genetically, I mean. Seeing as our closest genetic relatives are the chimps, and they are the animals that eat loads and loads of bananas. It must do something for your brain. Surely.

When Sweden Rules the World
by Patrick Gardner

ABBA brought us disco and still spawn catchy show tunes at an impressive rate. Ikea, the friendly furniture giant, won its way into our homes by serving up bookshelves and beds with a side order of... meatballs?

Platonic unisex saunas. Eccentric, blob-shaped cars. A wrist-slashingly morose national cinema, which nevertheless claims a cozy role as film theory's eternal darling. The mysterious Swedish bikini team.

Sweden, this anomalous, oblong nation of 9 million, wedged as comfortably as an axe into Europe's forehead, has enriched the world with a wildly disproportionate number of creations. Some nutty, some mythical, some not even Swedish at all – but many real and quite enduring. Most are easily consumable, charming, attractive, even downright sexy. Together they form an innocuous and palatable national image, which, had it been purpose-built to lull us all into cheerful submission, could hardly be doing a better job.

In our own sphere of digital advertising, Swedes are surprisingly omnipresent. For years, digital agencies and production companies with innocent-sounding names like Farfar ("Grandpa"), North Kingdom, Perfect Fools, Daddy, Great Works, and Acne – yes, that adolescent skin affliction – have topped the A-lists and racked up an impressive row of major prizes. While there is no official tally, a large minority of Creative Social's current members are also from Sweden.

All this when less than 0.15 per cent of the world's population is actually Swedish. What gives?

Although I'm an American by birth – born and raised in Oregon, about as far as you can get from Sweden and still be in the Western world – I've lived and worked in Stockholm since 1994, almost all of that time in digital advertising. Along the way I've had a unique chance to watch the Swedish digital industry grow from an embryo into a svelte teen.

These days when I travel I'm regularly asked: what exactly is going on way up there in the North? Why, for example, when a well-known American agency recently pitched out a new campaign for one of the world's top brands, were all four of the competing digital production companies from Stockholm? Is it something in the water?

The paranoid American in me is always tempted to joke about Sweden's secret push towards world domination. Is there something more sinister lurking behind that cool Scandinavian facade? Unlike most non-Swedes I've learned that the country, as recently as the eighteenth century, in fact, controlled much of continental Europe as well as a far-flung if modest colonial empire. They regularly fought head-to-head with the Russians, often to Russia's disadvantage. While Swedes are loath to admit it, many do harbor a secret nostalgia for this "Great Power" period in their country's history.

But in truth, I don't actually think Swedes are out to run the world. Luckily for the rest of us, that line of thinking is a thing of their distant past. Today's Swedes just want to do what they want to do the way they want to do it. Ironically, it's because of this fact that they frequently end up taking leading roles in whatever endeavor they set their minds to.

So what is it about the Swedish approach that's so uniquely effective, not least when it comes to digital advertising? Twenty years ago I studied a unit on "The Swedish Way" as part of a college comparative economics course. I still remember the textbook's bone-dry explanation of Sweden's success. *The rigorous exercise of democracy, careful compromises between capital and labor,* and *the good fortune of finding itself with Europe's only unmolested industrial base at the end of World War II* all enabled a unique third path between democratic capitalism and Soviet socialism.

Swedish social democracy seemed to offer the best of all worlds. National health care, generous vacation and parent leave, and other social benefits – even true gender equality. Together they helped yield long lifespans and a high overall quality of life. And all this was driven with jobs provided by successful multinational capitalist industrial giants.

But after arriving in Sweden, I found that my textbook was far behind the times. Swedes today work not within the system the book described but rather in that system's aftermath. Most of the great Swedish multinationals like Volvo, Saab, ABB, and Ericsson have either been sold off to foreign owners or have themselves chosen to move large parts of their operations abroad. National health care survives but its future at its present scale looks shaky. Sweden in the past thirty years, like the rest of the world, has drifted much nearer to democratic capitalism and can hardly be said to be on any kind of distinct third path any longer.

And yet the Swedish Way rolls on. Reformatted for the twenty-first century, Sweden 2.0 is in many respects just as successful as ever. At its core remains a set of principles that I have seen work well firsthand over my decade and a half here. In my view, these principles are what have probably always driven the Swedish story. They are the cultural factors that unite the many generations of Swedish success, including the era described by my old textbook, as well as our current one. These are:

1. Responsibility with freedom. This is the fundamental Swedish approach to work. Swedes work hard and require each and every member of the team to deliver. In return, as long as they live up to this tough ethic, they expect and generally get a degree of freedom to decide over their own work environments. It's not a free-for-all – just a tacit agreement and expectation that any responsibility given will be shouldered and a detailed task list is not always required to get things done.

One important advantage of this system, where every team member has the space and the right to think for him- or herself, is that it often allows the creation of unexpected but better solutions to broader team challenges. Another advantage is that it is possible to accomplish much more with fewer people than is common in many other cultures.

2. A willingness to stand up for healthy work–life values. As hard as Swedes work, they are equally demanding when it comes to their free time. With a state-mandated five weeks and often at least six weeks of vacation each year, plus a generous buffet of national holidays, Swedes take their time off seriously.

In my own native country, where people frequently have two or three weeks of paid vacation, many are still wary of taking even that much time out of the office, seemingly for fear of not having a job when they get back. A Swede would never think this way. In her opinion, any organization that would discriminate against her for taking necessary rest time away to recharge her batteries is not one worth working for.

Likewise, Swedes are willing to stand up to the powers that be to maintain a healthy daily balance. Parents will frequently leave work at four o'clock or even earlier in the afternoon to pick up their children from the country's excellent child-care system. And it is generally considered poor form to schedule or otherwise expect weekend work.

While all of this might seem to reflect a slacker mentality, nothing could be further from the truth. Swedes take their work very seriously – but they work to live, rather than live to work.

They recognize that without balanced home lives, they will be far less effective at what they do, they will fail in raising a healthy next generation, and moreover the point of all their hard work – living a good life – will be lost. The result: when a Swede does finally get down to work, she is charged, fresh, full of new ideas cultivated during down time, and ready to get things done.

3. Modesty. Swedish culture is self-effacing. Generally it is considered *fult att skryta,* which means "ugly to brag." In fact, Swedes (and Scandinavians in general, for that matter) take modesty almost to a fault with a phenomenon known as *Jantelagen,* or Jante Law, an unwritten rule that can be summed up with the statement "don't think you are special." Under *Jantelagen,* behaviour that even smacks of immodesty can be grounds for social ostracization. So it's no wonder Swedes take an understated, modest approach seriously.

While the latest generation of Swedes might be relatively brasher and more vocal than their forebears, they're still far more toned down than their international counterparts. Thanks to this, a wider range of voices, including those of many juniors, are able to come to the fore in the various ongoing debates. It also means that credit is often, although not always, given where it is actually due. The idea that successful hard work will in fact be properly rewarded is a big motivator.

4. Collabetition. Swedes are extremely competitive. For example, they love sports and excel at its higher forms, such as the Olympics. But as members of a small nation, they have also developed a keen understanding not only of the advantages but even the necessity of effective collaboration, of working together as a team with people of differing views and backgrounds in order to overcome challenges.

The result is something I've come to think of as *collabetition,* a system that is both collaborative and competitive at the same time. Collabetition exists both within and between organizations. Within a business, flat management structures enhance the personal sense of creative ownership and speed up information transfer between all members of the team.

Different Swedish organizations can also often be collabetitive. In some cases, even direct competitors will join together to tackle a shared challenge, allowing them to overcome together a hurdle each would have been too small to jump on its own.

5. Honesty, fairness, and mutual loyalty. Whether it is out of an inherent national goodness or simply because with its small population Sweden functions like a cultural island – where you know if you treat people badly you will have to face them on the street some day soon – Swedes tend to act decently in their business and other dealings. People speak their minds, lifting uncomfortable truths to the surface where they can be aired and exorcised more effectively, rather than burying their suspicions when they know something is wrong for fear of angering superiors. It is a country of verbal agreements, where deals are still sometimes done on a handshake, and even written agreements are far briefer than their foreign counterparts.

And finally, there remains in Sweden something that has been lost in many other places: a sense of compact or loyalty between employee and employer. When taking a job, an employee generally aims to stick with their new place of work for three or more years. Mainline employment is still largely full-time rather than contract based. And strict layoff rules generally keep employers from callously overstaffing.

All of these forms of honorable behaviour, along with many others, hold myriad benefits. Most of all they enable simpler, more rational, and at the same time longer-term choices on the part of everyone involved in the economic equation.

Honesty helps teams avoid unnecessary and costly mistakes. A simple legal structure makes life easier for businesses trying to get things done and individuals hoping to be treated fairly. And mutual loyalty means an employer can commit to long-term investments in employee training, development, and happiness, while employees spend less of their time searching for the next job and focus more on doing their best in their current one.

6. Innovation. Technical innovation has been a key ingredient to Swedish business success since at least the time of the great industrials like Nobel, Ericsson, Tetra Pak, and Saab. Today's Swedish digitals benefited in their childhood from the country's innovation tradition in many ways, including access to state-subsidized home computers (subsidies came through tax rebates) as well as high-quality, government-funded communications networks.

But Swedes aren't just technical innovators; they also have a long history of aesthetic innovation. Functionalism, modernism, and many other twentieth-century design and architecture trends had leading Swedish proponents. And the country's broad global reputation for quality aesthetics, as well as a cultural expectation of aesthetic innovation, were clear starting points for the more recent Swedish digital industry.

7. Acceptance of failure. Finally, if all of this so far makes Swedes sound like superhumans, take heart. They do in fact fail – pretty often, as it turns out. But here again a good cultural pressure-release valve comes to their assistance: a willingness to accept and learn from failure. While other cultures might blindly contend that failure is not an option, Swedes generally accept that some failure is bound to happen.

One thing that amazed me during my early years here was how utterly a Swedish politician might fail and still hold on to his job. What I didn't understand at the time was that in many Swedes' view, that politician had just become one important experience richer and was all the more valuable for it. Moreover, taking someone's career away from him is taking away his livelihood, something considered altogether too drastic for anything short of the worst crimes.

A similar mentality seems to run through most Swedish organizational culture. Failure is obviously not the preference.

But as long as it is honest and not repetitive, and especially if it is learned from, it is tolerated. Two great advantages of this are an increased willingness to take risks and a decrease in time spent worrying about losing one's job over making the wrong decisions. Both are powerful factors in generating positive results.

With all of the above in mind, Sweden might sound like some kind of impossible paradise, where great work springs purely from the sweat-free brow of ever-harmonious colleagues. None of that is true, of course. Sweden is an everyday place, much like any other, with its own shortcomings, such as rampant workplace politics, occasionally stifling conformity and narrow-mindedness, and even bouts of xenophobia. And as mentioned earlier, it also has its frequent failures, just like everywhere else.

But there are many elements of the Swedish Way that do make the country highly effective, and a number of these have also contributed to the success of Swedish digital advertising around the globe. And while Sweden's world-domination days are behind it, I for one hope the elements of the Swedish Way I've described do find their own way out and around the world, along with the great Swedish work that has proved so popular.

Despite cultural differences, these principles are just as applicable in Seattle, Singapore, or Sydney as they are in Stockholm. Sweden will never rule the world, but many aspects of the Swedish mentality do rule. And if you choose to, you can also make them part of your world today.

Here are my top ten tips to make your world a little more Swedish:

1. Work hard every day you work, be modest, and don't look for shortcuts.
2. Prioritize your private life, and refuse to compromise it away for work. If you need to, trade a higher salary for more time off.
3. Tell uncomfortable truths, and skip the jargon.

4. Always innovate. If it has been done before, do it differently or don't do it at all.
5. Collaborate, and give credit where credit is due.
6. If you've got that sweet corner office, turn it into your team's project room and move your desk back out onto the floor.
7. Keep structures and titles as flat as possible. You may need your title on occasion, but don't take it too seriously or use it as a wall.
8. Promote the doctrine that everyone contributes ideas.
9. Kill your darlings for the good of the project.
10. Cultivate a culture of responsibility with freedom. Let people know that they're allowed to fail, and don't punish honest failure.

FUTURE

Your Brand Is an Ape
by Chris Clarke

In the community age, brands must know how to behave if they want to be experienced.

David Ogilvy is quoted as saying, "the consumer is not an idiot; she's your wife." And yet for years the majority of advertising has patronised, flattered, and shouted its way to our attention from its protected position within a closed and arrogant media.

But we know that already. It's been said time and again by industry leaders from both sides of the digital fence. Yet rather like Mark Twain, who once said "reports of my death have been greatly exaggerated," advertising is not going to disappear. Neither will the rise of the internet kill TV, nor will mobile slay print ads. Viacom will not any time soon or in the future hand their lucrative outdoor sites over to Banksy and his mates. The future belongs to brands and agencies that understand that nothing new totally displaces the old. It belongs to smart creative thinkers who know how to create a coherent, compelling experience from the deracinated remnants of old media and the vibrant, shifting communities of the new.

For those seeking work in the agencies of the future, this offers huge potential – but only if they're prepared to give up the mono-media mindset that says it's all about TV and posters. It's not media innovation that has changed things; it's a fundamental shift in the behaviour and expectations of consumers. Two important principals govern creativity in our age: humanity and brand experience. Put simply, if you're going to enter into the social environment of digital communities, behave like a person who wants to be liked and in a world where no one media overrules another. Consider the experience your brand offers across channels, not just the impact of a TV ad. Writing this in 2010, a tipping point has certainly been reached, where most enlightened advertisers are thinking about engagement beyond broadcast, using social media to build advocacy with their audiences.

The internet has changed the marketing landscape. Online advertising has surpassed cinema, radio, outdoor, and TV in mature markets like the US and UK. And any marketer worth quoting in the pages of the trade press knows that consumers are now elusive beasts prone to ignoring most of the 3,000 ads they're exposed to each day.

So what's changed, then? It's all about consumer control. The web empowers individuals to control their media landscape as never before. With this control comes a lower tolerance of interruptive advertising and a greater demand for interaction. The implication for old advertising is clear: cling to the shouty, interruptive formats of the past, and be ignored; take advantage of the interactive potential of digital channels, and enjoy the spoils. With consumers congregating in communities, happy to disclose their most intimate secrets online, the new world is not impenetrable, and its denizens are certainly no brand avoiders. Rather, the role for brands is to enter those communities in a relevant, engaging, and human way. Like a bore at a party, talking endlessly about yourself won't win affection.

This gives rise to the fundamental difference between old and new forms of advertising. Where old advertising demonstrates the product proposition using actors or pictures, new forms help potential consumers experience the proposition for themselves. At its best, this new paradigm offers brands the chance to enter into or even create communities online, providing rich brand engagement, generating high levels of awareness, and shifting lots of product. Indeed, one of the characteristics of the new marketing is the erosion of the barriers between brand engagement and direct response. Why stop a consumer from making a purchase if it only takes a click?

Succeeding as a social brand is quite simple; it's just that companies often struggle with simplicity. Years of broadcasting messages have left businesses insensitive to the ancient principals of social engagement. It's the "you scratch my back, I'll scratch yours" principal inherent in all interactions between apes (ever watched chimps grooming?).

Known as the *value exchange*, this is the fundamental principle of the new marketing. This value exchange can take many forms. For some brands, the creation of deep, content-rich community experiences is not always relevant. In such cases – for example, in the provision of grudge purchases like insurance and utilities – the value exchange is all about relevance and convenience. A well-placed text ad within a search listing, leading to a seamless, easy purchase is all the consumer wants. In this instance, the role of the brand can be seen as the butler: discreet, there when needed, fast, efficient, subservient to your needs, and happy to bugger off as soon as the job's done.

Our lives would be fairly dull if we simply surrounded ourselves with willing manservants. In some instances, there is a chance to be the entertainer. In this space, there is and will always be a thriving role for TV-like video spots. Cadbury's fortunes were revived by a gorilla drumming along to Phil Collins in 2007, so the old TV format is doing well. But in a world where appointment TV is dwindling, spots must try harder than ever to entertain and will increasingly be judged by their star rating and view number on YouTube as much as by their on-air reaction. Some might say there's a limit to the depth of relationship you really want with a chocolate bar, and so it's appropriate for the entertainment to stop there for Cadbury. But in truth, there is a niche to be exploited online that can number thousands of motivated people. A visit to www.cadbury.com at the time of the gorilla-ad phenomenon yielded an opportunity to see the brilliant ad again, nestled amongst some truly awful design and a bunch of brochure-style articles about chocolate. How powerful would it have been to convert even a small number of visitors to Cadburys.com into loyal brand advocates prepared to convert others? So in spite of its success with the gorilla drummer, Cadburys had not yet created a brand experience extending beyond the immediate buzz of the spot.

As the connectivity between digital engagement and brand ideas has strengthened in recent years, models have started to become clearer. With the principal of value exchange in mind, smart brands have taken to looking at their target audience's behaviours and interests, looking for overlap with the brand proposition and then intervening in positive ways to amplify the audience's enjoyment. This is a fabulous way of maintaining relevance and even growing sales. In 2009 in Mexico, Snickers managed to grow sales by 14 per cent whilst the chocolate market shrunk 24 per cent, by using social media to create huge engagement around its sponsorship of the Urbania urban-sports event.

Similarly, Red Bull amplifies its "Gives You Wings" promise with deep involvement across a huge variety of alternative sports and Formula 1. Going beyond mere sponsorship, these kinds of events provide a brand with high-quality content to be exploited digitally.

Ever since the internet began to be taken seriously as a marketing medium, we've heard the phrase "content is king." Looking to the future, this will only become more apparent. For a while in the noughties, it was possible to engage digital audiences simply with interesting novelties of interaction. As the web has become more and more a participatory medium where technology is less of a differentiator, interfaces have been simplified, whilst audiences focus more on the content itself and the people they share it with. YouTube, Facebook, and the countless WordPress sites reflect this.

Beyond the provision of content, a world of opportunity has opened up for brands that want to offer services, tools, and functionality. Branded utility, using the means and the creativity available for advertising to create a promotional service, looks set for major growth in the next decade. Platforms like Nike+ and IBM's Wimbledon utilities aimed at their corporate audiences, and innovations like Fiat eco:Drive all point the way towards marketing as a service. The huge expansion of iPhone apps in 2009 provided brands with easy ways to offer utilities that could impact consumers on a daily basis. Kraft's iPhiladelphia recipe app, Vodafone's provision of cross-platform mobile experiences as part of their F1 sponsorship, and Absolut Vodka's Drinkspiration cocktail app are great examples of brands being helpful in your pocket.

In a world of climate crisis and increasing awareness of the impact of our lifestyle on the planet, a new burden is placed on corporations and brands to make a difference. This opens the door to some fruitful forms of value exchange where marketing budgets can be put to good use improving the world we live in rather than simply cluttering it with ad messages. American Express have done just this with the Members Project, a digital brand experience designed to re-invigorate the notion of membership, which has always been the cornerstone of the Amex brand. With a pledge to donate $4 million to a good cause chosen by its members, American Express turned the idea of marketing expenditure on its head. Rather than talking about themselves, Amex was able to demonstrate the power of membership through the interests of its members. The campaign leveraged "traditional" channels to drive awareness of the activity, but the centre of gravity was very much the online experience where members and potential members could suggest and vote on worthy causes.

Here was a major corporation recognising the need to create experiences beyond the broadcast message, allowing consumers to express their interests while the brand presents its message in a relevant way. The winning project will provide clean drinking water to communities in Africa. How fantastic it would be if other major brands could spend a proportion of their budgets in this way, creating a virtuous circle of marketing objectives, consumer interests, and corporate social responsibility!

Perhaps the best opportunity for expansive creative thinking offered by the digital world is in the field of *alternate reality games* (ARG) - interactive narratives that use the real world as a platform, often involving multiple media and game elements, to tell a story that may be affected by participants' ideas or actions. Here the brand really can operate with a personality, combining the roles of entertainer and motivator, and ending up as an elusive trickster. Perhaps the most famous example to date has been the launch of the Batman movie *The Dark Night* from 2008. Pioneering agencies like Entertainment 42 set up by ex-Microsoft executive Jordan Weisman have been innovating in this space for years. With the advent of 3G mobile networks and the interactive capabilities of devices like the iPhone, it is likely that the rich interplay between the physical and virtual worlds offered in ARGs will become an increasingly important way for brands to cut through with certain tech-savvy audiences.

Entertainment 42's client, alternative-rock band Nine Inch Nails, developed a massive ARG to promote their new album. Frustrated by the limited opportunities for expression offered by digital-music formats like MP3, lead singer Trent Reznor wanted to create an experience that would truly engage his fan base. The ARG itself is so big and comprised of so many different media types that it's impossible to figure out alone, so by its very nature it taps into the collaborative power of digital communities, creating a great deal of conversation and massive buzz around the band. Whilst this approach requires huge commitment from the communicator and the participants, it continues to grow.

In a world of consumer control, brands are learning the humility to behave more like people than didactic organisations. Those that get it right provide a powerful value exchange based on a real understanding of what they can offer relative to their audience and communication objectives. Such brands are able to create engaging brand experiences with the potential to enrich people's lives. In a future where advertising has to work ever harder to capture attention, the role of brand communication, and specifically the creative task, will become ever more important. But the creatives who succeed need an ever broader range of skills, from the writing skills needed to create eye-catching TV spots, to the business acumen to spot the opportunities for branded services such as Nike+, to a deep understanding of how consumers engage with different devices and media. The job's never been harder, nor more worthwhile. And for those hungry enough, the door is wide open.

Is Peep Culture the New Pop Culture?
By Chris Baylis

When was the last time you spent an afternoon mooching around Facebook catching up on what your friends have been up to? I bet it was more frequently and recently than the time you watched a whole movie, sat in front of the TV for an evening, or watched so-called branded content online. As we dedicate more and more of our time to peeping in on other people across social media, is this just another form of competition for brands, or can brands use peep culture to connect with a disparate audience?

Here's another question for you. How many friends have you got on Facebook? How many followers on Twitter? Have you ever wondered how many friends are too many? According to anthropologist Richard Dunbar, the answer is anything over 150.

This number, known as Dunbar's number, is a theoretical limit to the number of people a person can maintain stable social relationships with, in relation to his or her brain size. Chimps have a Dunbar number around 50, and this number gets smaller as you descend down through various apes and their corresponding brain sizes. For us, with our large cortexes and other spongy bits, the number of people we can maintain *meaningful* relationships with is 150. This can be seen recurring across history and sociology; 150 was the basic unit size of professional armies in Roman times, and 150 is often cited as an appropriate size for a modern company. Actually, take a moment to think about it. Try and think of 150 people who you know and like. For some hypersocial people, the number will be bigger; for others it will be smaller.

Back to chimps. Picture a chimp doing chimp-like things – not wearing a bowler hat and drinking tea, but picking bits off another chimp while he in turn has bits picked off him. This communal grooming is important far beyond basic hygiene. Chimps groom much more than they actually need to because it's a way of being social, staying connected to the group, and sharing information.

As humans evolved, we replaced grooming with language, which is why gossip is actually very important to maintaining the social health of communities. This used to take place over the garden fence or at the water cooler. But as society has become more atomised, so has gossip over the garden fence fallen away. Who actually knows their neighbours anymore? The paradox is that we all have hundreds, if not thousands of contacts across online social networks – but we often don't know our neighbours.

So what's going on? First of all, it's easy to see that virtual gossip has replaced actual gossip. Sharing of photos, status updates, and GPS locations creates an ambient intimacy that could easily be looked upon as a new form of grooming. And as our lives have become broader and more global, information relevant to our social groups is not local information about Mrs. Miggins at number 30; it's whatever happens to be the social currency of our particular networks.

As an expat, I've found myself spending what is probably an inappropriate amount of time on social networking sites keeping up with old friends and acquaintances. I still like the fact that the bloke who I worked with couple of agencies ago who played really good music on the office stereo still shares the odd find on Facebook. I get to keep all the best bits of our relationship without any of the actual effort of meeting him for a drink regularly and picking his brains about his latest music finds. However, I also miss out on a regular pint where we discuss music and perhaps other more meaningful things in life. But let's face it. Who has the time for more than a handful of "real" friends?

Dunbar states that most people have a core of around five real friends – people we are genuinely intimate with and would probably help us hide a body if push came to shove. From here, friends pan out in rings. As intimacy drops off, quantity and connectivity rises – until we end up connected to that girl from school we quite liked but who now lives in another city and we will never actually meet in real life. Dunbar questions the value of these contacts and states anything over 150 is simply voyeurism. But is it as simple as that?

What is the reason you're still connected to that guy you met at a conference three years ago or that person you were quite good friends with twenty years ago but would barely say hello to if you ran into her in the street? It's perhaps a symptom of what Alain de Botton calls "status anxiety." There is genuinely status to be had from how many people you are connected to on social networks. But is this just a sad number you can virtually wave in people's faces like a pack of Top Trumps, or is there some value in having lots of connections? The answer is a bit of both.

For example, if I were to hire a strategist within my agency, would I choose one who has 150 followers on Twitter or 1,500 followers? All other things being equal, including the freshness of their breath, I would hire the person with the most followers. The reason being is that we live in a connected society, and volume is influence. A strategist with a large network will be more tuned in to what's going on, and he can canvas opinion, change opinion, and even help recruit better people. Having a wide network actually has real value beyond the mere showing-off value of the number itself.

Let's turn this around. What makes a person worthy of connecting to? What makes somebody friend material on

Facebook (whereas he or she may not be in real life), and what makes somebody worth following on Twitter? Or to boil it right down: why would I peep in on someone in the first place and carry on peeping?

The people worth peeping in on know something we don't or do something we can't. They have created some piece of content, albeit 140 characters, that we find interesting, entertaining, or relevant. Or they've gathered some piece of information first – a YouTube video, an app, a link – or perish the thought: a piece of branded content or branded utility.

But we need to include an important distinction here. *People don't connect to share; they share to connect.* We want to share popular culture to make us the centre of our networks and to gain influence, kudos, and status and bring us into contact with new networks – the joy of a re-tweet being the best example of this. Like chimps, we want to groom more than we need to. We want to spend as much time as possible around the water cooler gossiping, whether we like to think we do or not.

Different networks share different things, of course. Going back to Dunbar and his rings of friends, the reason we have rings of friends of varying social distance is that the more disparate people we know, the more networks we become a part of. So keeping in touch with the girl I went to school with or the guy I met at a conference is worthwhile because it opens up more networks as these people act as interconnecting nodes. (It's worth dipping into the work of Clay Shirky if you want to brush up on your network theory.) Given that different networks will peep in on one another for different reasons and share different culture, this actually makes me quite influential if I am a node between groups; I will cross-pollinate culture from one network to another.

Peep culture isn't replacing pop culture; it's influencing it. Word of mouth is more immediate than ever when it comes to movies, TV, music, and new technology. As soon as a new piece of hardware comes out, we will all be following the trending topics on Twitter to see if it sinks (#fail) or swims. Google Wave, anyone? No, thought not.

But what about advertising? Shareability is now a common feature in most advertising briefs. Social seeders will become a new discipline in advertising agencies in much the same way as planners did in the 1970s. Planners were psychology students who abstracted the target audience into research, data, and insights. Seeders will be sociology students who DJ at the weekends and regularly hang out with the target audience or can network with and influence people who do connect with the target audience.

As agencies we are helping brands catch up with this thinking. I imagine we all regularly tell our clients that if they want to exist in this space, they must be relevant, interesting, useful, or entertaining – which in theory should make them likeable and therefore shareable. The other thing we try and tell them, in as nice a way as possible, is that no one wants their plonky advertising messages landed in the middle of our social networks. Not only will people not share the message, they will actually reject it out of hand and socially ostracise the brand responsible. People will not be peeping in on the brand, to say the least.

For me, one of the most interesting home pages on the internet is Flickr. It actually says on its home page, "'Share your photos. Watch the world." As one of the most successful brands online, their reason-for-being actually sums up the whole notion of peep culture: share and watch. Perhaps the only thing missing is rate and influence, but this is implied. What this ultimately means for brands is share or don't share, buy or don't buy. It's as simple as that. If you're not well liked and therefore not well shared, you may as well pack up and go home now. Simply being on a social network will not get you peeped on. You have to be so much more.

So is having any more than 150 friends too many? I say the more, the merrier. Of course, you can hardly play the networking influence card when rummaging around in people's wedding photos online, but connections and internetworking give everyone a chance to influence all the peepers out there. A peep quickly becomes a share, which in turn becomes a moment of influence. The more influence, the more we eventually get what we want. Which is what?

Well, that's up to us to decide. If we want environmentally responsible companies, the influence of our networks will start outing the villains and praising the worthy. If we don't want another *Pirates of the Caribbean* movie, we hope that the highly social movie-going audience will force the franchise to walk the plank. There should be nowhere left to hide for modern brands as we peep in on them and share their good behaviour and bad in equal measure.

And of course, brands should be peeping in on us. Social networks should become brand listening stations. We should be defining the behaviour of some of the biggest corporations out there; not just social, environmental, and commercial behaviour, but physical behaviour as well. It used to be the case that big beat small. Brands with the highest spends who could shout the loudest won the day with old-fashioned, frequency-based advertising – i.e., buy lots of media space and repeat. This is becoming increasingly irrelevant. Big no longer beats small; fast beats slow. The brands that will come out ahead will be the ones that respond the quickest to microtrends and shared memes and be the first to have a presence on the latest social networks.

We've all been trying to explain to our clients for some time that the rules of the game have changed. Some get it; some had it and have lost it. Quite a few are still trying to find the right change to hop aboard the magic bus. Peep culture will redefine popular culture. Everyone with a network will, whether they do it consciously or not, leverage their ability to rate and influence what we think of as the good, the bad, and the relevant.

The Filter
by Flo Heiss

Hi there. How are you? Been online today? Uploading images? Writing on your blog? Yes? Thought so.

Have a good look because what you see is the old internet. It's changing in front of your very eyes. Something new is growing: a new web that isn't a web anymore, but an organism, a brain.

What?

We are busy filling the web with information, experiences, applications, stories, emotions, and connections. Data. We are all helping to build the most comprehensive, up-to-date, ever-changing data brain on Earth. And what's more, the internet is not constrained to that screen, that box in front of us anymore. The Net is migrating onto handsets and bleeding into the real world.

The internet is not about the internet anymore. At last.

We are creating this collective brain because we can. Because we like to. Because it's in our nature and because it's fun. But with all this data online, on mobiles, and offline, how is anyone going to find anything anymore?

With so much competing noise, it is very important how brands cut this data, how it's being accessed, and how relevant "nuggets" are presented to the user. Here's the thing: I believe that those nuggets will come to us via RSS, friends, intelligent neighbouring serendipity algorithms, suggestions, and conversations.

This means the way to access this data will be more akin to a filtering through the vastness of this brain. We need a Filter on the old 2.0 web. A meta web that sits around the old web like a halo or onion skin. This new brain is being fuelled by the fact that the current static internet protocol (IP) address structure of the web with unique universal resource locators (URLs) for sites is also changing as we speak. We no longer access content through a unique URL; instead we have unique IP addresses for each piece of data. There will be an infinite number of unique addresses available, so each thought, image, word, and pixel will have a unique address.

When was the last time you typed a URL into a browser? Static web addresses will lose their relevance and their value to marketing. Imagine each brick of a house having its own postcode. How are you going to say where you live?

The consequence of all this is that traditional online advertising will lose its importance. What surfaces on the Filter will be conversations about your product.

Our opinions, thoughts, and feelings will replace advertising messages. That's why it's vital to have a good product – something that people like to talk about. Good agencies understand that, and create content that comes through the Filter. Content that's free, new, useful, and funny.

"Do you want to know what the Matrix is, Neo?"

Alternate reality applications, Earth maps, and simulators will have evolved into a parallel universe, pretty much like *The Matrix*. Imagine Google Map's and Earth's content and interface being updated at twenty-four frames a second. What you will see is a live version of our planet. And everything is clickable.

On the 2.0 layer, there will still be unique URLs campaign sites and traditional online advertising. This place won't be visited very often though. The place to look to advertise is on the Filter.

But how do we do this since there is no digital real estate for sale on this level? We need to create marketing that surfaces on this layer. We won't buy brands as entertainment; we want products that entertain. We want things to connect with and engage with. This means we need to look at a new type of marketing. We need to work *with* clients and not *for* them. We need to develop unique and exciting products with our clients. Good products don't need to be advertised; the Filter will find them for you. Knowledge about great products flies around the globe in no time. Good stuff will surface on the Filter.

In addition to that, we can see a trend of the digital bleeding into the real world. The recording of our lives through 2.0 and other experience storage applications is being combined with position awareness. This effectively means that we are recording the present for the future. Our mobile device becomes the remote control to navigate this world and read what's around us now and in the past: the stories, sounds, and images someone has left for you to pick up. We are busy creating a time machine. You can go back in time to see what has happened here years ago in context of the place.

My son will be able to know what he did 1 March 2010 at 16:34 because I made a record of it and stuck it online. The better the recording devices become and the faster we update this parallel universe, the more realistic our trip back in time becomes.

"Time circuits on. Engine running. Flux Capacitor... fluxxing. All right!"

—Marty McFly, *Back to the Future*

All this, of course, is free – an open source that is up for grabs. I do believe that everything digital will be and should be free.

So how are brands going to make money? If you want your brand to still matter in fifty years' time, you need to put all the emphasis on having a great product. And that's what consumers are prepared to pay for. We are prepared to fork out for real things. The more digital our world becomes, the pricier live experiences become. Theatre, art exhibitions, live music – we will pay for all of them.

Live is going to be expensive. Everything digital will be free – unless we start charging for the Filter, of course....

"The revolution will not be televised; the revolution will be live."

—G. Scott Heron

Get Involved: How You Can Shape the Future of Digital Advertising
by James Cooper

I have a confession to make. I have been a creative director for three different internationally admired digital agencies, won lots of awards and worked with the biggest brands in the world, and I couldn't tell you what the difference between a JPEG and a GIF is. I have spoken at conferences around the world and written for the most high-profile publications about digital and websites, but I wouldn't know how to actually make a website if my life depended it. I also have a blog and write frequently about the future of digital marketing when, truth be told, I have no idea what is going to happen next. What does this mean? That I'm a charlatan. No – well, maybe – but let's not go into that here. No, what this means, what this actually proves, is that you can be a success in digital without being a nerd or a geek, without really knowing the first thing about computers. What this also means is that because our world is in a constant state of flux, it is never too late for you – whoever you are – to make a successful career in digital marketing.

The digital marketing industry is full of contradictions, hot air, and hyperbole. If someone working in the ad industry, agency or client side, had pulled a Robinson Crusoe or Tom Hanks and lived on a desert island for the last fifteen years, returning now he would be forgiven for thinking that the whole world had changed and that his skills were completely useless. "No digital experience? No technical knowledge? You don't have an RSS feed that talks to your refrigerator? Forget it." This is nonsense. But it's nonsense that has been created by the press and the digital industry. In my opinion, there are three reasons why the role of technology has been exaggerated over the years and has been used, by some, as a barrier to pushing the whole industry forward.

First up, the whole dot-com boom and bust. This was a classic *Revenge of the Nerds* scenario. At the start of the boom, it was cool to talk up your tech credentials and exaggerate everything to stupid proportions. Everyone was doing it, despite a lack of actual knowledge. And ad agencies were very keen to get in on the action, pitching for silly dot-com businesses that were always doomed to fail. And fail they did. End of part one.

We then had a second situation where many digital agencies were fighting for economic survival and had to go on the defensive. Jargon was used as a defence mechanism, and a few people started acting like stroppy teenagers. For example, a digital person might say to a traditional agency or client, "God, you don't know what ASP is or why this needs to be done by a .net person?" (For the record, neither do I.) "It just does OK? That will be 200k, please." Desperate times called for desperate measures.

The third reason that everyone started exaggerating the tech aspect – which actually still happens today – is due to some of the incredible money behind tech IPOs. If in the nineties you didn't have any Netscape stock and then you somehow managed to miss out on any Microsoft stock and more recently Google, then, well, you were a doofus – or at least made to feel like one.

The end result was a deafening techno babble that was a load of hot air, but no one had the balls to call it.

I honestly feel that these three points have stopped some great people from trying their hands in the industry. No one, let alone people who work in advertising – where show and bravado have traditionally been all – wants to look stupid. No one wants to admit that they don't understand things. It's perceived as a sign of weakness. We need to stop that. As I said, I've been doing this for years and still don't understand – or want to understand – the engine under the bonnet. It really doesn't matter. We need to stick to the things that we are good at. So if you're a creative, focus on coming up with a great idea or mastering your craft; if you're a planner, a great insight; a client, fostering a relationship where great work can flourish; if you're an account man, well, just make sure you have change for the cab. In one sense, of course, this is business as usual.

Think of it this way. Our Crusoe or Hanks ad exec probably commissioned hundreds of TV or print ads before she got marooned – actually, she was probably on his way back from a shoot in Cape Town. She would have understood the process intimately: brief, presentation, budget, production. That hasn't changed in years. But unless she was a real film buff, she would have had no idea about the specifics of a TV shoot. There was no need for her to know what a gaffer does. There is actually no need for anyone (save perhaps the art director, at a push) from the agency to know these things either. The point is so long as the TV ad looks good and there are doughnuts at the shoot, everything is cool. So it must be with digital. It doesn't matter if you don't know what a SWF file is; it's irrelevant, as long as you're confident that someone in the team does. This confidence is the key to success: being able to leave things to other people so that they can get on with doing a great job (and not worry about it).

So, if you don't need to have technical knowledge, what do you need to have? I think you need to have an empathy with the digital world and an understanding of the possibilities the technology gives us, if not the actual mechanics. I've had many clients who simply refused to believe that real people had the time to customize sites, upload pictures, comment on blogs, post tweets, and so on. As marketers, they spent their whole days in front of computers so that they couldn't see that for someone who works outside of our little clique, actually coming home and getting an email about a YouTube clip or mucking about on Facebook is fun. It's relaxing after a hard day's work; it's entertainment. I took some clients away for a day and forced them to make their own blogs. Yes, even a Luddite like me knows how to set up a blog – and that's the point. After thirty minutes, they were uploading photos of themselves and watching silly movies of one another. So my advice would be to at least dabble in some form of the digital space, as this will help you grasp some of the possibilities.

The other important thing is to be aware of some of the consequences. Take something like RSS feeds. Now again, I don't really know how these work, but I do know that they mean that people are aggregating their preferred information onto one page or device and that people are not using portals like MSN or AOL like they used to. Furthermore, I know that this has huge implications for future marketing plans. Some would argue that Twitter has overtaken the need for RSS feeds. But again, you don't need to know why this is happening or how – someone can do that for you. Just be aware that the digital marketing world is, as we like to say, in beta – constantly changing.

In the same way that you shouldn't fret the tech, this flux shouldn't deter you either. The web and digital marketing are still in their infancy. Although the first banner appeared in 1994, essentially banners still exist in the same shape and have the same "click here" message. OK, we can put video in, search boxes, web functionality, and so on, but the result is very much the same. The thing that has changed is that banners along with websites are no longer what digital marketing is all about. We now have blogs, social networks, viral, virtual worlds, widgets, and a whole new ball game with location-based mobile content.

The point is, I have no idea what the next big thing will be. Some students in California or just as likely Stockholm, Shanghai, Warsaw, or Tel Aviv will be working on something that will flip things again, but it's pointless trying to predict what these things will be – unless you're a venture capitalist, which you're not. You're in the communications business.

Think about tech aspect from the consumer's point of view too. Recently there has been great debate within the tech community over whether HTML 5 or Flash will be the dominant platform to develop content. Amongst some people, this debate will rage and rage for the next three or four years. For the record, and to help you look a little smarter at dinner parties, HTML 5 and Flash are both ways of making content come to life on the web. HTML 5 seems more suited to mobile content such as iPhone apps. But how about the consumer? In reality, they couldn't care less whether you make your cool, whizzy video thing in HTML 5, Flash, or CupCakes (not real); they just want a great experience. They will never look under the bonnet either.

For every Facebook, YouTube, Twitter, or Foursquare, there are ten platforms or ideas that some media agencies will guarantee clients is the next must-have. Don't waste your time second-guessing this stuff. Concentrate on getting your head and your structures right so that when something interesting does come along, your organisation – whether you are a client or an agency – is ready to go. Be flexible, nimble, and fluid, not just with your process but also with your media budget. By the way, this means experimenting and the whole thing about experimenting is that things go wrong. This is a good thing. That's how Post-it notes were made.

As I have said, what comes next is anyone's guess. But one thing I do know is that for every crackpot who claims to have invented the future or disgruntled nerd who puts up the techno frighteners, there are thousands of very clued up people more than willing to help you figure out stuff. The great thing about the web and our community is that people actually get a kick out of helping (you don't think I'm getting paid for this, do you?). What this means for you is that if you're serious about kick-starting a digital career or trying a little experiment, it's never too late. I really believe that a two-week crash course with someone who knows what he's talking about, a couple of reads of this book, and some regular blog reading would give you the requisite knowledge to be part of a digital campaign that was either award-winning or hugely successful in terms of sales – and, who knows, maybe even both.

One final point: even though it really is never too late, there's no time like the present.

Brands as People
by Benjamin Palmer

I've got a secret plan. I would like to make brands act as much like people as possible.

When I was a kid, I read in the encyclopedia about how corporations are structured. I learned that initially it was a sort of application process; the government would dole out a charter, an official sanction to do business. The rules and laws for a corporate charter were very different from the rules and laws for people. At a certain point, though, some enterprising corporate heads found that they liked the way the "people laws" worked a bit better than the corporate laws, and they successfully petitioned the American legal system to give corporations very similar rights to a human being. This soon became the norm across the first world. It's pretty interesting. Look it up; I did.

So when I read this as a kid, in my childhood imagination all the big companies and brands in the world were aiming to be just like real people. They wanted these laws because they were the multinational version of Pinocchio, desperately trying to be a real boy. I imagined the boardrooms staffed by folks who maybe didn't feel like a whole person on their own, so they joined a corporation and collectively made up a human being. I assumed the big boardroom discussions were about making big decisions on how to act more people-like and what to do next, pulling the levers in the machine like Metropolis.

Cute, right? Well, obviously not really the case, but it's also not far from becoming a reality. Here I am now – a grown man, business owner, internet creative marketing guy – and I think that the idea of brands acting like people has become probably one of the more pressing needs for brands today, entirely because of the internet.

We are here at the dawn of the social web. The game-changing technologies on the internet at the moment are the ones that let us comment on the world in as many ways as we can think of: from broadcasting our moment-to-moment status, location, or opinion to commenting and tagging not just every digital conversation and content, but the real world as well. In 2010, this is new but it's also such a natural extension of our human behavior that soon enough it's going to feel like this is what the internet was always meant for.

The transformation we are going through at the moment in technology is moving from the interactive version of "old media" – publishing, television, and so on – to a digital version of our behavior out there in the real world. We are also bringing the internet out of the house. It already seems antiquated to log on to the internet or find your way to a computer to access the web. We've always got it with us, and because we have access to everything and everyone all the time, in many ways we don't even realize we are online anymore. Big companies, brands – our clients – now have to figure out how to behave in a time when, just like all of their customers, their every move is observed and broadcasted, accepted or rejected. That's branding in real time on the social web. It's totally freaking everyone out right now, which is actually pretty awesome because transformational panic usually leads to great things.

Last century, when I was just starting out building sites for big companies, there was an unexpected psychological turning point as brands built their first presence on the web. It was the innocuous-sounding section called 'About Us." At the time it was one of the de facto pages on every website, where you could say hi and introduce yourself and talk about what you were all about. It was a great opportunity to show your character as a brand. You could be friendly or fun or smart or impressive – it was a good section for a website! And it induced sheer panic in a lot of companies. If you think about it, they had previously never had to tell the general public what they were about; outside of the occasional mission statement or annual report, there was literally no place before "About Us" where a brand had a whole page devoted to talking about itself. So it was a big identity crisis and a source of much discussion and argument and "coming soon" pages.

Of course, over the years brands have worked out what to put on that page and what to do with websites in general. The corporate home page is now sorted, but of course the internet will never be static. Social media has now replaced "About Us" as the biggest worry for corporations.

At the moment there is another panic afoot, and it's a little more complicated. Let's call it "How Do We Behave?" It's a much more complicated proposition this time around. Now it's about brands figuring out how to be interactive.

So ironically, now there really are a bunch of folks in a room at all the big companies trying to figure out how to act like a real person. Pretty awesome. It's actually necessary too, because as the online world is becoming the dominant form of media, huge swathes of the online experience are being built for people, not brands. In some ways, the brands have to adapt to the conversational habits of their customers when they're operating in a medium built for the people.

I'm pretty excited that this is real. Perhaps it's because I started off thinking that was actually true, that big companies were trying to be more like us. But here we are today. The populist technology of the internet has won out, and we find that brands have to start learning how to be more people-like in order to meet their goals, instead of imposing their messages on others.

We, as the occasional or permanent stewards of a brand, are in a pretty influential and responsible position of what we're trying to get brands to do and how we are advising brands on how to act. We're constantly setting the tone, and when any new form of brand behavior is successful in one way or another, it's emulated over and over.

I really want brands to be disarming, to be more normal. To live up to the human aspirations that are part of their heritage. To integrate with us and be as dumb and smart and socially responsible and friendly as you or me. I figure that things will work out better if all the people in this industry feel like it's not only OK to be human about it, but it's actually the goal.

Behavioural Economics and What Lies Beyond

by Mark Earls

Technology is the most marvelous thing: not just for what it does or even what it enables us to do but also for what it reveals about us and who we really are.

Four hundred years ago, optical lenses were the technology du jour. When combined together in pairs (enclosed in a simple wooden tube), these slivers of seventeenth-century Silicon Valley greatly increased the distance a pair of human eyes could see – from at best a handful of miles to the almost unimaginable distance that the stars in the night sky seemed from us. Not only did this "telescope" enable individual astronomers to see things previously unseen – new planets, moons, and comets as yet unimagined – but when deployed by an eager distributed user base from the Thames to the Danube making disciplined observations of the movement of the heavens that we were not who we thought we were (or at least, we did not sit where we thought we did which was almost the same thing): far from being the centre of the universe (and thus of God's creation), this simple technology demonstrated that we sit in the cosmological equivalent of a rusty lock-up on an abandoned industrial estate on the edge of a forgotten provincial town in the land that time forgot.

And this uncomfortable little insight into our place in the universe in turn kick-started a whole flood of social and political changes on which our modern world is built – things like democracy, for one. No simple ground lenses, no internet, if you like.

A very similar thing is happening today: the technology that we in the digital world are exploring is telling us some pretty important things about ourselves and helping us redraw the map of what it is to be human and how human behaviour is shaped and spreads. For example, for much of the last two or three centuries, we've been taught that what separates our blessed species is our ability to think independently, using our powers of reason to shape our own destiny. This is – or should be – the proper way for humans to behave: collect and weigh the information, and then make a rational choice about what to do. Rene Descartes, Adam Smith, and my mother all agreed: think before you act.

But anyone who has spent any time working in the digital space knows that the last thing you want people to do is think about something; you want them to do stuff. Too much thinking, too many clicks and you've lost the user. Far from being the rational deliberator of received wisdom, digital teaches us very quickly how lazy most humans are. To paraphrase Daniel Kahneman, the spiritual leader of the new discipline known as *behavioural economics,* humans are to thinking as cats are to swimming: we can do it *if we really have to,* but we'll do all we can to avoid it. And, as the fantastic personal financial confessional *A Mathematician Plays the Stock Market* by John Allen Paulos (one of the world's greatest mathematicians) shows, all of us are subject to a host of cognitive biases and tics that distort our view of the world and lead us not just into temptation but into trouble time and time again, however rational our thinking and precise our calculations are. Paulos lost his shirt on investments in stocks like Enron and WorldCom due to the biases and errors built into the design of his all-too-brilliant mind.

Working in the digital space throws up evidence of this kind of insight into human behaviour all the time. Perhaps this is why it is those with a keen interest in digital who most fervently champion the books and the papers that behavioural economists are writing (take a bow, Rory Sutherland). What's more, if you're looking for better insights into human behaviour to shape your work and its effectiveness, you could do a lot worse than dig into the larder of wisdom and insight that is behavioural economics (I particular like those easy-to-use lists of biases and quirks).

And yet, all is not as it should be in the digital garden. Too many of us are still using ideas about human behaviour transposed (uncritically) from the old world. Take, for example, the notions about influentials and influence being peddled by the social media gang. On the one hand, the science is quite clear that most human social networks are *not* structured in the hub-and-stroke way that the influential hypothesis would require; on the other hand, things are a lot messier in the real world on- and offline. Influence is often mutual and many-directional. It's not a one-way street, like some kind of human-enabled information micro-broadcast system!

These qualms aside, folks who are working in digital are already doing much of the heavy lifting in charting the next version of the human map – the one that goes beyond seeing us as either calculating robots (that classical economics suggests) or quirky, miscalculating ones (that behavioral economics describes). And this is all about the *social.* As a community, we've already demonstrated how fundamentally social human beings are through the widespread adoption of the connective technologies we have championed and our attempts to create contagious content and behaviour to spread across the social systems these technologies enable. Without this noise around the social side of digital media, much of the science that I and people like me have been championing would not have gained the general currency it has in mainstream advertising, in business, and in society at large. You wouldn't be reading, as I seem to do almost daily, that *it is now widely acknowledged that we are fundamentally a social species*. For this, I thank you all.

But the next step is to help the rest of the advertising world and society at large to really understand what it means for humans to be fundamentally social. All too often I get the impression that when I talk about this idea, what folks take away is the idea that humans like going out to bars a lot (which is, of course, true but only a small part of the argument), but at heart they're still independent creatures.

No matter how much science is published (and republished and reinterpreted by folk like me)—science that repeats this "social idea"—it's only by folk like the digital community developing ways of talking about and interacting with humans as social creatures, individuals embedded forever in complex social systems, that the rest of business and society at large is going to be able to get to grips with the science and what it tells us about ourselves.

And you thought digital advertising was just a fun thing to be doing, eh?

Being Good
by Johnny Vulkan

"Pass the milk please, dear," replied the woman while deftly sidestepping the seemingly easy question being posed to her. "So, remind us again what exactly is it that your son does?"

It was slightly disturbing to discover that someone's mother (OK, my mother) would actually be slightly embarrassed that her child worked in advertising, but upon even the most cursory examination she does have a point. Advertising and marketing, in all its forms, doesn't have a particularly good reputation (a moment's pause for irony, please). It's sadly not a new thing, nor is it one that has escaped the attention and occasional amusement of authors, film-makers, and the popular media.

We can start back in 1957, where the American journalist and social critic Vance Packard wrote the million-selling pop psychology book *The Hidden Persuaders*. With it he raised several moral questions by lifting the lid on motivational research and the ways in which it was being applied to "manipulate" people.

Skip forward to 1978 and the BBC radio and TV comedy series *The Hitchhiker's Guide to the Galaxy* by Douglas Adams.

Fans will recall the planet Golgafrinchan – an advanced and philosophical society apart from the one-third of their population that they realize served no real purpose – hairdressers, management consultants, telephone sanitizers, and yup, of course, us marketing people.

Another decade on and in 1990 Dudley Moore stars in *Truth in Advertising,* where his patently ludicrous idea that advertising should be straightforward and honest sees him incarcerated in an asylum. Then 2001 sees Tim Hamilton's witty video shorts of the same title expose what we all secretly thought. Its endlessly quotable script is maybe best summed in a line delivered by an agency producer: "I can't wait to make this blight on humanity."

The year 2007 saw an appropriately brief release for the critically panned *Perfect Stranger.* It starred a sharp-suited Bruce Willis as Madison Avenue's most powerful advertising executive who also just happens to be a murderer. At least today we have *Mad Men.* Chisel-jawed Don Draper, building bonds with clients, fiercely defending his creativity while working his way through the women of the series. Oh dear. Ah well, the suits and setting look great, and like most of the above, it does make for great entertainment. But it's hardly the stuff of heroes and role models, and we have only ourselves to blame.

Somewhere along the way our industry's brief to present products and services in a compelling way to people became subverted into a game to convince people that real men smoke and if you occasionally can't sleep at night you should ask your doctor about prescription Hypochondriax™.

And it was a fun game for many ad folks while it lasted, but that game has run its course and rightly so. It's been replaced by a new, improved digital version. The question is, are the rules the same? I suspect, but more importantly hope, that they're not.

The generations born digital have a unique opportunity compared with those that preceded them because of a very simple shift: the world of commercial communication is no longer one way. This is not the place to wax lyrical about the pros and cons of social media, citizen journalism, crowd sourcing, or any other descriptor inclined to cause venture capitalists to salivate, but this is the place to talk about an important side effect of our new emerging digital dialog world. It's called "the truth," and you'll be pleased to learn that a lot of good things come with it.

The detractors out there may cry foul here. "Truth, you say – it's just a lot of people whining through their keyboards." I beg to differ. Sure, a few belligerent mudslingers exist, but that's democracy for you and you need them to make the rest of us look sane.

For the first time in human history, an unprecedented number of people have the ability to give constant feedback to any company on any topic at any time, whether those companies would like us to or not. It is this dynamic – the ability to research and question, to publish and provoke – that leads to the truth, because lying, skimping, shirking a responsibility, or denying a truthful allegation is simply no longer an option. You'll be found out. Just ask the makers of the Krypton bicycle lock.

And this is all great news for society. The result should be good products made by good companies who offer them at fair prices to people and communicate them in a decent and honest way. Gone should be the days of mediocre, "me-too" items wrapped in a thin veneer of communication metaphors and analogies. Replacing them will be a market for innovative products and services, clearly differentiated and offering real value.

That's great news for the marketing industry too. While technology has created a whole new set of tools for marketers and birthed some of the most exciting new companies our industry has seen, it's actually also made our jobs easier. Better products and services require us to simply connect people to them rather than batter them into submission or worry them into purchases. Technology has very kindly taken "good" from a moral "nice to have" to a business imperative.

An oversimplistic prognosis? Of course, but optimism is another splendid side effect of the digital age, so let's run with it.

But being good in the digital age isn't going to be just about making better products and marketing processes that stand up to interrogation. It's also about how we're going to behave as individuals going forward, and that's going to be a little harder.

We're only at the second bend of the dot-com roller coaster, and I imagine there are as many dips as climbs on the rails ahead. The issues we face are as much about society as they are about marketing; our fates are intertwined. Data permeates almost every aspect of first-world life, and as data-driven companies look to give their services for free – from music to phone calls to email and search – they're still looking to the same people to foot the bill: advertisers. And in return for that funding, advertisers expect to get that data.

There are potentially big positives to this. It should mean fewer, better messages coming our way as potential customers, but the question does remain: will it? The fact is that I really *do* know what you did last summer; your data vapor trail will tell me. I can increasingly find out what you did in the last few minutes. But just because I know, does that mean I have a right to use it?

The debates around privacy and data are nothing new, but they have certainly accelerated and are become more pointed. New advertising models from Facebook to Google skirt the blurred edges of what many people think is acceptable. On top of this, the impact of rapidly increasing levels of mobile and location data will push these questions even further.

So what will we do? Our industry has a choice. But far more importantly, we as individual practitioners have a choice.

Being good in the digital age is not going to be about one single big idea. It's going to be about a long tail of goodness. It's about the everyday cumulative little moments and decisions made by each and everyone of us – the "pleases" and "thank-yous," the moments of reflection and invention and increasingly the moments of restraint.

It's about realizing that we're all allowed to think and act beyond our job descriptions. It's about asking questions and interrogating long and hard enough to make sure we're comfortable with the answers we get back. That's not somebody else's responsibility; it's ours.

I can't make those choices for you, and neither can your company, college, or school. We each have to make our own, but I hope that when you do it's one you make while thinking about your mother because we've got all the data on her too. Maybe the decision will be different from the one you'd make if you didn't.

Agency of the Future
by Daniele Fiandaca

In the advertising industry, there have been four significant periods of change. On the back of technological change – nationally networked television on the one hand and full-colour printing of photography in print media on the other – the sixties saw the birth of a new advertising model, led by DDB (Doyle Dane Bernbach) in the US and CDP (Collett Dickenson Pearce) in the UK. In this new model, it was believed that great creativity led to greater impact, which led to more effective communication. Then, in the eighties, we saw the emergence of media independents such as CIA and Ray Morgan and Associates, which led to the later split of media and creative. The nineties marked the emergence of the planning agencies, such as Naked and PHD, while the noughties will be remembered for the emergence of the digital agencies.

But despite all these changes, the underlying business model has remained pretty much the same. Not any longer.

Massive changes in the wider media world, driven by the internet, have altered our world forever. Brands can no longer rely on shouting at consumers with TV commercials to guarantee success. If the product is not differentiated or the customer services fall down, you can shout all you want: no one will buy. Conversely, some of the biggest new brands, such as Google, have been built without recourse to traditional mass marketing at all.

It's not as if we weren't warned. In 500 BC, inadvertently Confucius predicted the future of marketing communications when he said, "Tell me and I'll forget / show me and I'll remember / involve me and I'll understand." This is the basis for the future of our industry.

From now on, advertisers need to concentrate on delivering a minimum of one of four things to consumers (the four Es):

- Education
- Entertainment
- Engagement
- Exchanging Value (which incorporates utility)

I believe that this is going to require a fundamental shift for most agencies, and unless they adapt, they are soon going to find themselves extinct as margins continue to erode and their product becomes far less relevant in this new connected world. To do this, they are going to need to be able to think beyond just single disciplines and instead focus on delivering ideas that generate demand for their client's products and services through one of the four Es. As Bill Bernbach famously said, "Properly practiced, creativity must result in greater sales more economically achieved."

Obviously, it would be impossible to know exactly what this agency of the future will look like. If I knew, I would be spending the next few years building it. The reality is that those agencies that truly succeed and define the next decade will all look slightly different and will adopt their own personal product. However, I do believe that many of these agencies will share some, if not all, of the following ten characteristics.

1. Digital at its core

Okay, so you might expect this in a book written by digital peeps. However, it is fundamental: the internet has driven changes in consumer behaviour. Online's place in the overall consumption mix is only going to get more marked as the current crop of *digital natives* (anyone under twenty-five who has grown up with digital technologies) grows older. Digital natives see no barriers between the real and the virtual worlds. A friend can be someone in the same street or someone in the same network. So, for many new consumers, digital is not a channel or even media; it's a part of life. How, and where, marketers engage with consumers is more important than ever because they have never been more adept at avoiding the advertisers they dislike or mistrust.

What this means is that agencies need to have people who live and breathe digital. In addition, the skill sets needed to meet this challenge in the digital world are far more complex. You can no longer rely on a creative team to come up with an idea, write a script and then simply pull in a production company to deliver it. There is not such a clear gap between the idea and implementation. Now, it's highly likely that a digital advertising campaign will involve a planner, an art director, a copywriter, an action scripter, a designer, and a creative director – all equally responsible for bringing the ad to life. There is no doubt that the best campaigns in the marketplace are now totally integrated, and this is simply going to bring more people into the mix.

2. Return to full service

We will see a return to full service but not as we know it. It will be made up of three core elements: creative, creative media, and creative tech. Creative departments will no longer be the preserve of the art director–copywriter team but will rather consist of people who simply have great ideas, whatever their background. Yes, there will still be room for skill-specific arts (such as copywriting, scriptwriting, typography, and so on), but they will not be the heart of the team.

Media will not be about mass media buys; that can be left to the big media-buying beasts. What we will see is far more creative media – the type of planning that is currently being done by the likes of Naked, as well as the full-service digital agencies. In addition, the agency will be tasked with distributing content in nontraditional ways, such as via peer-to-peer networks. Media solutions will become far more about engaging communities than mass reach campaigns, and agencies will bring in conversational specialists to manage these conversations.

Lastly, creative technology departments will build applications and widgets that will provide value to people, both in the physical world (Nike+) and the digital world (Uniqlock or MySkyStatus). Providing this will require a different mix of people, as agencies such as Anomaly are already demonstrating.

3.   Connection back to customers

I have had comments from a number of marketers saying that agencies seem to have lost touch with the people they are meant to be connecting with in their advertising. For example, digital media became central to people's lives long before traditional advertising agencies woke up to its importance. Creatives need to get much better at really understanding the relevant target audiences, walking in their shoes and thinking the way they do. At my old agency, we would always try and bring people into brainstorms who represented the target audience. When we did we invariably got better, more relevant ideas that really connected.

It is also worth noting that in this context I have avoided the use of the word *consumer*. I believe that the word *consumer* is the most overused and misleading word in communications today. How often are we speaking to our client's target audience when they are consuming? And how impersonal is the word *consumer*? I wonder how much truth there is the quip from a senior creative who recently said to me, "We call them *consumers* to make us feel less guilty about selling to human beings." I would love to see the industry referring to *customers* or *people*.

4. More strategic suits

I am not, however, suggesting that the agency of the future is overrun by planners who spend all their time understanding the audience. Rather I think the agency of the future will have far more strategic account people who can not only "manage" the client but will also have a complete understanding of the client's business and audience. They will undoubtedly get support from some specialist planners who are able to bring some key insights into a brief, but ultimately the suits will become the owners of the brief at a strategic level, as well as being the client liaison.

5. Independent spirit

Independence breeds creativity; it is no coincidence that independent agencies are so successful at awards time. This does not mean that the agency of the future is not part of a network. But those networks must ensure that their agencies retain an independent state of mind. The signs are that this is already happening: when, for example, WPP bought Clemmow Hornby Inge, the management of CHI retained 51 per cent of the ownership, replicating a model that has clearly worked well with BBH and Omincom. Expect to see far more deals of this nature in the future, as the networks realise that the buy-out model is ceasing to work (with the unfortunate demise of Farfar being a perfect example).

6. A global view

We can learn a lot from one another, and there is no doubt that the internet is enabling this at a greater rate than ever before. We saw the phenomena of a website in Korea called Cyworld (founded in 1999) way before the emergence of sites such as Bebo, Facebook, and MySpace. In China there are currently over 50 million people who have a pet within QQ pet (an online version of Tamagotchi mixed with social networking), while over

100 million people are playing the online dancing game 9you. Japan historically has led the world of mobile, and innovations like QR codes, two dimensional bar codes which can be read by mobiles using their cameras, were implemented way before they arrived in the West.

However, one of the biggest change factors is going to be the fact that for once US global marketers (which represent nearly half of total global marketers) are suddenly aware that the US is no longer their dominant market as a result of the growth of the BRICs (Brazil, Russia, India, China). Consequently, their marketing solutions need to be far more locally culturally relevant, and they will need to use an agency that can tap into these cultures. This will require a different sort of global agency – one that has access to global talent without the barriers that exist in a network agency.

7. Egolessness

In this case, I am referring to ego in relation to notion of self-importance or self-image rather than in the context of the "I." It is this concept of egolessness that is probably the biggest difference I have seen in the digital sector as compared to the traditional world. Moreover, it's one of the reasons that Creative Social has been such a success. It really hit home only when a traditional creative director spent two weeks in my old agency and gave me his first impressions: "I am astounded by the egolessness in the agency. I could not tell you who the bosses are. More importantly, I can see in the brainstorms that there is a complete openness to listen to ideas irrespective of their department or seniority." In fact, egolessness is one of the pillars of creativity, along with perspiration, abstraction, emotional skill, and social environment.

Although it is hard to define the best possible physical manifestation of this, in my experience, an open plan office tends to be a good indicator of a culture with few egos.

8. Being good

I am not going to cover this in detail in this chapter, as Johnny Vulkan has covered it so eloquently in his own essay. However, there is no doubt that it's going to become far more important for agencies to ensure that we're being good. This goes beyond simple pro-bono campaigns (which we all know have been done for less altruistic reasons: i.e., pro bono = award-winning potential) but will need to be part of an agency's core values, which will be driven from those at the top of the organisation. It will also determine which type of clients those agencies work for as well as the type of work that they do.

9. Collaboration

I think the way agencies will work together will change significantly. Clients need to be demanding that their agencies work together in a far more integrated fashion. This may mean bringing in the best people from each of their respective agencies and asking them to work together in a far more collaborative way. It was interesting to hear how closely Crispin Porter + Bogusky works with Burger King's other agencies and that the actual idea for BK Games originated from Burger King's PR agency. The fact that Crispin Porter embraced it and made it such a success is tantamount to a new level of collaboration.

It was interesting to see a brand like MINI in the UK appointing two digital agencies on their account despite a relatively modest budget – the result being one gold and two silvers at Cannes in 2007. I would also not be surprised if we see examples of direct competitors working far more closely together. If we truly want to provide our clients with the best solution, why not call a competitor to see whether we can utilise one of their teams that we know includes the best comedy writers in the industry?

10. A new financial model

Finally, I noted at the beginning of this chapter that the most significant change in the advertising industry was the move from commissions to a fee-based model. Now the next step needs to be for us to be paid based on value delivered, as opposed to one based on time.

The agency of the future will have some of the most creative and intelligent people in the world. We need be looking to allow these people to deliver ideas that can be used either for advertisers (existing clients or new clients) as well as in other stand-alone ventures. As well as delivering on existing briefs, the agency should be thinking up ideas and taking these to clients and charging them on a royalties basis – whereby the more successful it is, the more the agency receives in the form of fees. This can equally be in the form of content, product design, or extension to the existing brand. Additionally, I would expect agencies to come up with their own ideas that they can execute and grow themselves. In other words, agencies may well become media owners, looking to engage with clients as partners in new ventures. Interestingly, some agencies have already launched their own IP divisions.

Undoubtedly, new models of payment will evolve that should allow the agency of the future to retain far more control of how much margin it retains in that it will be far more the master of its own destiny. Fortunately, this has already started to happen. Anomaly has already set up as a different type of agency that is not scared to become a record company, and it often takes equity in the venture rather than fees. BBH has set up Zag, Naked has created Naked Ventures, and Great Works has created Great Works Innovation. It is going to be interesting to see what products/businesses come out of these businesses in the future.

Whatever happens over the next few years, I have no doubt that the industry is going to have to evolve significantly and it is going to be fun to be part of that process. I do look forward to seeing who makes that leap to becoming the agency of the future, although as architect Nicholas Negroponte once said, "Any agency which describes itself as an 'agency' does not have a future." So maybe that agency of the future will not be called an *agency* at all...?

A Blast from the Past from the Future
by Gavin Gordon-Rogers and Gemma Butler

We missed the deadline for this book. Way too much pitching, and clients always comes first. Luckily, thanks to the wonders of modern technology, it's now possible to send data back in time (for an exorbitant fee). Of course, all messages are strictly monitored and censored so as to avoid the very fabric of the space–time continuum unraveling. So much as we'd like to, we can't tell you when to bet on Arsenal winning the Premiership. Well, we can, but you won't get to see it. It's in ██, and ██, and ██.

Anyway, we thought it would be worth submitting a little piece for consideration even though we're several decades late. But what should we write about? Naturally, the other essays in the book have already covered a wide territory. And let us tell you, *Digital Advertising: Past, Present, and Future* has for years been one of the cornerstones of marketing practice for students, marketeers, and brand leaders. What more can we add, other than to give you a brief snapshot of how it all turned out….

So what's changed here in 2030? It's difficult to know where to begin. What is marketing? Do agencies still exist? Do consumers care? Is the Semantic Web working? Has digital made the world a better place?

Let's start with what's closest to our hearts: our own necks. What does the agency of the future look like? The situation can be summed up in one word: *diversification.* Fortunately, agencies still exist but they now take far more diverse forms and include the following: creative technologists, who are the new artists; intelligent personality-profiling companies that also deal in data privacy; games developers who create brand experiences; professional brand evangelists; parallel world builders, designers, actors, and traders; the new form of ▮▮▮▮▮▮ based on the principles of ▮▮▮▮▮▮. The list goes on.

The point is that, as asserted elsewhere in this book, the "traditional" model of brand communication is totally dead. That doesn't mean that traditional media is dead. Agencies still produce TV ads (IPTV, contextual bumpers, and so on), newspaper ads (digital readers), and billboards (digital billboards). The agencies from 2010 that have succeeded are the ones that have consistently been most open to evolution.

It's claimed that Charles Darwin said, "It is not the strongest of the species that survives, nor the most intelligent, but rather the one most adaptable to change." Whether or not Darwin said it, that was and still is something for all agencies to live by.

What about the concept of all our data forming a living, growing brain, and what Flo Heiss refers to in his essay as the "Filter"? Thirty-one years ago (1999) Tim Berners-Lee, inventor of the World Wide Web, foresaw the evolution of our use of and access to data: "I have a dream for the Web in which computers become capable of analyzing all the data on the Web – the content, links, and transactions between people and computers. A 'Semantic Web,' which should make this possible, has yet to emerge, but when it does, the day-to-day mechanisms of trade, bureaucracy, and our daily lives will be handled by machines talking to machines. The 'intelligent agents' people have touted for ages will finally materialize."

Between fifteen to twenty years ago, people started to become overwhelmed by data and all the different possibilities data offered. The first iterations of data filtering – RSS feeds, personalisable home pages such as iGoogle, Twitter groups, and so on – were simply not intelligent or advanced enough to cope. New services were developed hand over fist, many of them by brands. Only a few of the very best ones won out.

Today, most people use ████████ from Google. Acting as a filter is just the start of its capabilities. It categorises, associates, contextualises, and summarises all our data. Wherever, whenever. Best of all, it learns to know you. It even prompts you: to buy things; to get in touch with people; to take a break, have a kip; to take a vitamin pill; to go on holiday or change careers. Depending upon how you react, it learns and changes its behaviour; a virtuous circle is created. Ultimately, it doesn't just know you – it *is* you. Your alter ego, alive and well, skiffing the data oceans. Happy sailing.

One of the most crucially significant (and most enjoyable, both for marketeers as creators and for end users as consumers) areas of development over the past twenty years has been gaming. Where once consumers might have watched a TV ad or visited a campaign microsite, now they can fully immerse themselves in a playable parallel world where the brand controls every tiny detail.

Advergaming (or brandgaming) properly began in the early years of the millennium. It was starting to take off around the time that this book was published: branded console games, interactive cinema trailers, the sharp rise of 3D in cinema accompanied by the launch of the first 3D home cinema screens. Webcams built into screens as interaction controllers became the norm quickly. Fully interactive movies where you play the lead role and can affect the plot with every decision you make – these are now ubiquitous. Augmented reality contact lenses (ARCs) have become a genuine consumer proposition rather than being readily accessible only to the military. MMORPGs (massively multiplayer online role-playing game) swiftly morphed into MMARRPGs (massively multiplayer augmented reality role-playing game).

We learnt how to play the advergame the hard way when we created our own MMARRPG *Monster Munch Mayhem* back in 2022. The concept was simple, in theory. Put on the free ARCs that came with every twelve-pack of Monster Munch and watch, in stupefied amazement, as the Pickled Onion Monster bursts forth from your packet of Pickled Onion flavour, reshaped baked corn snacks. Your adventure begins…

The aim was to befriend as many monsters as possible – which was, of course, easier when you used unique codes on the packs – in order to build a personal army, compete with others, and ultimately defeat the synthbots and their evil overlord. The always-on, 4D nature meant that, in essence: you snooze, you lose.

Before long, perfectly well-adjusted eight-year-olds could be seen in playgrounds, embroiled in epic unseen battles, wildly gesticulating at thin air, screaming gobbledegook spells at one another, and collapsing in shell-shocked, eye-bagged exhaustion as the end-of-playtime bell rang out. It was quite wonderful. The nation was hooked. And not just kids – nerds too. Even a few real people. *Monster Munch Mayhem* was in full effect. Sadly, the industry didn't quite take the same shine to it. The media were outraged. One rag wheezed that it was "cynical, corrosive, and morally bankrupt." PepsiCo (owners of Monster Munch) were losing a lot of money too, what with all the ARCs they were giving out. The servers were switched off at the height of *Monster Munch Mayhem's* popularity (which only fuelled its subsequent cult status). Game over.

Insert coin.

With the advent of new types of sensory tech came the opportunity to make immersive brand experiences ever more realistic. Taste, smell, touch – including temperature, pain, and so on – all delivered via data streams. Every visceral detail conjured into life by nanobots and chemical arrays and nervous system stimulators and mind-control interfaces.

These parallel worlds are currently massively popular, not least because they afford the user *real* escape into an aspirational, beautiful, safe fantasy land where almost anything is possible. It's like Second Life to the power of all your senses. Some of the most popular, like Pringles Pop Till You Drop Party Island (by glue London) and the Official Ferrari Gigolo Experience (by AKQA) have years-long waiting lists. Others operate on invite-only policies.

But there is one thing common to all the successful branded worlds, and in fact, one thing common to *all* successful brands in 2030: Accountability. Honesty. "Being good," as Johnny Vulkan puts it in his essay on page 133.

Has digital made the world a better place? Undoubtedly.

Has *digital marketing* made the world a better place?

What we have learnt is that brands are alive, like people are alive. They need to behave well – to be not just accepted by society but befriended. The brands that didn't grasp this failed. Those brands that were style over substance. The brands that undertook morally questionable activities or dealt with unethical partners and financiers.

Now, because all information is open, brands must choose their principles wisely and stick to them. Consistency of character is as important in a brand as consistency of value or quality of product.

So. We didn't promise some kind of special recipe for success from the future. Even if we had it would have been censored. All right, let's have one more go. The winning numbers for the world's biggest ever lottery jackpot, an eighth rollover week in the Euro Millions draw on Friday 25 January 2019, are: ■, ■, ■, ■, ■, ■ and ■.

There is no secret formula.

It's really as simple as it ever was. The brands that people really care about are the ones that stand for something. They invite their customers in. They are open. And they tell a damn good story about their beliefs.

Be good, and good luck.

Appendix: Author Biogs

Alessandra Lariu, SVP Group Creative Director, McCann Erickson – New York

Before McCann, Ale worked at Agency Republic in London – four times Agency of the Year – and before that Framfab/LBi. She has won many industry awards, including Campaign, D&AD, CLIO, and OneShow Interactive. Ale grew up in the Amazon jungle in Brazil but in 1990 swapped monkeys for computers. Ale has been obsessed with all things digital ever since. She is the founder of a group for women in digital called SheSays, which has over 3,000 members. In 2010 Ale was elected the twenty-ninth most creative person in business by *Fast Company* magazine. And she is one of the geekiest women in advertising. Follow her @alelariu.

Anders Gustafsson, Creative Director, Crispin Porter + Bogusky – Europe

He's the only non-founding CD in the history of the agency (which was originally born as Daddy) with past and present clients that include Scandinavian Airlines, Heinz, Volkswagen,

Red Bull, and Ikea. Anders has been in the industry for over ten years, during which he completed a full circle from traditional to interactive to integrated advertising in all media. He is passionate about contemporary art and music. And he is a kick-ass guitar player. Follow him @agcdcpb.

Andy Sandoz, Creative Partner and Innovation Director, Work Club

Andy is one of the original partners of Work Club, founded in 2007. Previously he was CD at Agency Republic, a TV channel brander, a designer, a 3D animator, and originally an illustrator who got frustrated that his airbrush did not have CMD+Z. He's passionate about the internet as a power source for business and social change. And he tries to smile in photographs because people tell him he looks grumpy, which makes him grumpy. You can follow him on the streets of South London or @sandoz.

Benjamin Palmer, Co-Founder and CEO, The Barbarian Group

Benjamin Palmer is co-founder of The Barbarian Group and has served as its CEO since the company's start in his apartment in 2001. He has been named one of Creativity's fifty top creatives and one of *Esquire*'s Best and Brightest. In addition, The Barbarian Group has won Digital Agency of the Year several times, as well as many international awards. Benjamin leads the creative and cultural vision of the company, overseeing creative as well as the agency's overall direction. And he's terrible at making cocktails but is excellent at drinking them. You can follow him @bnjmn.

Chris Baylis, Executive Creative Director, Tribal DDB – Amsterdam

Having started out in the late nineties at Profero, Chris partnered with some wonderfully crazy art directors at Agency Republic before an award-winning stint on Audi at GT. An irresistible offer in 2007 saw him hot footing it from London to Amsterdam, where he now runs Tribal DDB. Currently best known for creatively directing the Grand Prix–winning "Carousel" (aka "the crazy clown film") for Philips, Chris enjoys judging, speaking, and a spot of lively debate at events from Rio to Cannes. And like every writer in advertising, he still dreams of finishing a novel and has even tried his hand at stand-up comedy. Tune in @chrisbaylis.

Chris Clarke, Chief Creative Officer, Lost Boys international

Chris has worked in digital since the late nineties, drinking his morning coffee at Abel & Baker, Wheel, Modem Media, Digitas, and now Lost Boys international (LBi), where he is responsible for creative in sixteen countries. During this time he's won awards at Cannes, D&AD, IAB, BIMA, LIAA, NMA, Marketing, and Campaign. He now judges at a number of shows, where he can be found throwing chairs around and shouting "next!" (in a nice way). In his spare time, Chris writes fiction and poetry. He got pissed off signing up for Twitter so chose @golansleepweed as a name. He now realises that the joke's on him.

Daniele Fiandaca, Co-founder, Creative Social; Founder, Digital Fauna

Daniele Fiandaca is currently running his own consultancy, Digital Fauna, as well as working on numerous projects with some very good friends. Previously he ran Profero for over a decade, growing it from a small team in London to the global business it is now. He also continues to run Creative Social, which he founded alongside Mark Chalmers in 2004, and he has sat on a number of juries including D&AD, Festival of Media, M&M Europe and Revolution. Daniele's passions include film, collecting vinyl toys, and traveling to exotic places. He also starred in an Italian TV commercial for a karaoke magazine when he was eighteen. Follow him @yellif.

Dave Bedwood and Sam Ball, Creative Partners, Lean Mean Fighting Machine

Sam and Dave have been a creative team since 1995. Fortune more than foresight saw a move to digital in 1999. Since then they have been captivated by the unlimited opportunities afforded by digital. The year 2005 saw them pick up Campaign's Young Achievers of the Year Award, and their UK peers voted them the number-one creative team in digital, an achievement that has graced every biog thereafter. Since starting Lean Mean Fighting Machine have won a whole bunch of awards; their proudest moment came in 2008 when Lean Mean Fighting Machine were the first ever UK agency to be crowned Interactive Agency of the Year at Cannes. As a youngster Dave used to play for Aston Villa, whilst Sam starred in a TV commercial for Atora suet. Follow them at your own risk @dbedwood and @samuelball.

Fernanda Romano, Global Creative Director Digital and Experiential, Euro RSCG – Worldwide

Fernanda started her career as a client at Schering-Plough in Brazil but soon moved into advertising at Euro RSCG in Brazil. She left after a year, joining internet start-ups and returning to advertising only in 2000 at DDB Brazil. Since then she has worked at JWT in London and Lowe in New York and Madrid, before rejoining Euro. She's won several industry awards, including medals in Cannes, One Show, and NYF. Fernanda watches the three *Godfather* films once a year – all in the same day. You can follow her @fefaromano.

Flo Heiss, Creative Partner, Dare – London

Flo Heiss was born in deepest Bavaria and grew up in a place called Murnau. Yes, that's right – a place where people actually wear lederhosen. Flo is the creative partner at multi award-winning agency Dare in London. Dare was voted Campaign's Agency of the Year in 2003, 2004, 2005, and 2007 and Digital Agency of the Decade in 2009. Flo has chaired and sat on numerous international juries, including D&AD and The One Show. He studied graphic design in Germany, in Italy, and in London at the Royal College of Art. He also has an unhealthy obsession with animated GIFs and giant squids. Follow him @floheiss.

Gavin Gordon-Rogers, Executive Creative Director, Agency Republic

After studying film-making at Edinburgh College of Art where he was BAFTA nominated, Gav directed music videos for artists such as Belle and Sebastian and Paul McCartney before becoming an advertising copywriter in a team with his wife, Gemma. They worked at traditional agencies for several years before "digitising" into glue London in 2002. They then moved to Republic in 2005, where they were instrumental in developing the agency's creative reputation. Gav's passions include zombies, Haribo, Leonard Cohen, red wine, and his family. At aged eleven, Gav used to write his own programs in BBC Basic in order to test his Latin vocabulary. Follow him @gavrog.

Gemma Butler, Creative Director, Agency Republic

Gemma was a conceptual artist and art directed and built the sets for Gav's music videos, turning Scotland into the Wild West and churches into secret gardens. They later became a creative team and worked at "above the line" agencies, including Circus and Karmarama, for several years before moving into digital at glue London. Multiple awards later, they moved to Republic, where they created two of Campaign's top ten digital ads of the decade. Gemma is passionate about her rumbustious daughters and how much they sleep at night. And she is (very) loosely related to Jackie Onassis.

Gustav Martner, Partner, Executive Creative Director Crispin Porter + Bogusky – Europe

Gustav is a digital re-inventor, media-agnostic creative, and skinny Swede in tight jeans who co-founded Daddy at the turn of the millennium. One year later, the agency was named Online Agency of the Year in Sweden. In the decade to follow, Daddy expanded whilst maintaining its presence in Sweden's top echelon of digital agencies. In 2009 the US-based creative powerhouse Crispin Porter + Bogusky acquired Daddy, turning the agency into its European hub. Besides working hard with this venture, Gustav likes to play with his punk band and hang out with his wife and kids. And they also wear tight jeans.

James Cooper, Creative Director, Saatchi – New York

Campaign described James as "one of the brightest stars in digital advertising." His first ad was a terrible TV spot for Somerfield but since going digital things have got better. Having been the creative director for Dare and Agency Republic in London, a partner at Anomaly in New York, and now CD at Saatchi New York, James has racked up some impressive awards and even more impressive name tags. He also founded *Celebrity PingPong* magazine in 2008. Yes, that's right: ping-pong. Find out more @koopstakov.

Jon Sharpe, Chief Digital Officer, M&C Saatchi Group

Previously Jon founded two of the UK's leading digital advertising agencies, Itraffic and Play, and was managing director, digital marketing at Agency.com. Prior to advertising, Jon studied English at King's College London and Cambridge University. His passions include food, funk, and football. Jon has released obscure records that the music press said nice things about but not very many people bought. Follow him @jonsharpe73.

Johnny Vulkan, Co-founder and Partner, Anomaly – New York

Starting his career in London, Johnny has lived and worked in New York since 1999 and is one of the architects of Anomaly, rated by *Fast Company* as one of the most innovative companies in the world. His role covers digital and media innovation as well as emerging commercial philosophies. Johnny never has less than three cameras with him and is the proud mayor of twelve venues on Foursquare...this week. You can follow him @johnnyvulkan.

Laura Jordan Bambach, Executive Creative Director, Lost Boys international – London

From humble beginnings as an interactive artist and trained taxidermist, Laura cut her teeth as a key figure of the infamous "geekgirl" hyperzine in the early 1990s. Moving from sunny Sydney to London, she's held senior roles at Deepend, Lateral, I-D Media, and glue before heading up the reigns at the LBi mothership with her partner, Simon. She travels a lot, speaking about ideas and geeky stuff that take her fancy. As well as her day job as an award-winning creative lead and ruthless optimist, she is founder of SheSays, a global network encouraging more women to put down their ponies and pick up a computer. Laura once led a mass wee on stage, but don't worry – it was all in the name of performance art. Follow her @laurajaybee.

Mark Earls, Founder, HERD consulting

Mark Earls is a recovering account planner whose HERD consulting is at the forefront of understanding and applying leading-edge behavioural and cognitive science to help marketers understand and shape human behaviour more effectively. Previously, Mark worked in agencies radical (St Luke's) and just plain big (Ogilvy Worldwide) but is much better now (thank you). His writing is widely read and awarded: e.g., his latest book (*HERD*) explores human behaviour through the lens of what science tells us about our fundamentally social nature. Mark has to keep working to pay for his sad addiction to English cricket. Follow him @herdmeister.

Matt Powell, Creative Director, Profero – London

Matt originally trained as a book designer and spent a whole year creating an Atlas of World History. Opening the finished hardback in a store, the first thing he spotted was a typo. He turned to digital and joined Profero where he still works today. Over the last decade he has worked on brands such as Channel 4, Johnson & Johnson, and MINI but is most proud of a succession of government campaigns protecting children on the internet from predators and cyber bullies. He is highly awarded and been on a number of juries, including the Cannes Cyber Lions. Matt tries to spend as little time in London as possible but fails spectacularly at this on a weekly basis. Follow him @observatron.

Patrick Gardner, Co-founder and CEO, Perfect Fools

Fool that he is, it might come as no surprise that Patrick started his career as an assistant speechwriter to US VP Dan Quayle in 1990 and 1992. After working with traditional marketing in the US, Mexico, Russia, Indonesia, China, and Sweden, Patrick went digital in 1995, co-founding Houdini Digital Creations in 1999 and Perfect Fools in 2002. While he enjoys living and working in Stockholm, he shares the Swedish passion for regular escapes to explore the rest of the world, preferably with family. And as a former child model, Patrick once placed second at a nationwide competition in New York (there were two male contestants).

Rafa Soto, Creative Director and Founder, herraizsoto&co

Rafa started his career as a copywriter in BBD Barcelona and Publicis Barcelona. He then took a break from advertising and worked as a scriptwriter for Spanish TV. In 1997 he fell in love with interactivity and its narrative capabilities and started herraizsoto. His agency is today one of the most awarded in the country and manages clients such as BMW, Ikea, Camper, Guinness, Diageo, and Carrefour. Rafa actually started his career when he was nine, singing a jingle for one of the cheesiest commercials ever for hair lice. Yeah, hair lice. Follow him @rafasoto.

Samuel De Volder, Creative Director, These Days/Wunderman

Sam, thirty-seven, started as a copywriter and concept creator in 1996. In 2000 he became creative director at These Days, Antwerp, where he works together with a bunch of talented craftsmen and women to create integrated work with (in most cases) an interactive backbone. He won awards and judged CLIO, New York Festivals, Cannes Lions, and so on. Sam enjoys reading (now crunching *Washed Meat* by Thomas Rosenboom) and running (Nike+: sdevolder). Sam is married and is the proud father of Natan, Quinten, and Ada. And he takes pictures of his own shadow, but he does not know why. Follow him @sdevolder.

Simon Waterfall, Founder, fray

Simon Waterfall is currently running around defending creativity with the energy of a weasel on crystal meth whose tail has been slammed in the door of a 1972 Capri Mk II. His company fray was set up at the beginning of 2010 as a vehicle to carry the fragility of a design concept through the various barriers of its life cycle, from product design, branding, advertising, and beyond. Previously he was a founding partner and creative director of Poke and Deepend, is a past president of the D&AD, and is a BAFTA member. In 2009 he was awarded the title of Royal Designer for Industry. He loves the sound of his own voice but until the age of thirteen couldn't spell his middle name. And he needs your help.

Lightning Source UK Ltd.
Milton Keynes UK
UKOW051903170613

212391UK00003B/648/P